My Surprise Family
Find Your Ancestry Story

Margaret M. Nicholson, PhD

My Surprise Family
Find Your Ancestry Story

MS MARTIN ADVISORS LLC
St. Augustine, Florida
2018

MS Martin Advisors LLC
24 Catalonia Court
St. Augustine, FL 32086-7679

Publisher's Note: This is a work of non-fiction based on the experiences and memories of the author. Others involved may have a different view of a situation or conversation. With few exceptions, names are accurate and used with permission. Family trees have been adapted for purposes of relevance and privacy.

"How To" anecdotes and the Sections represent the author's personal use of a public Website. This information is not meant to represent a comprehensive manual or a replacement for the company's support center to which readers are encouraged to get up-to-date instructions.

Web addresses or links contained in this book may have changed since publication.

Email comments or corrections to:
MySurpriseFamily@gmail.com

ISBN 978-1-7326389-0-7

LCCN: 2018914820

Author: Margaret M. Nicholson, PhD
Layout Design: Heritage Designs LLC
Cover Design: Christy Sheffield Sanford

IN MEMORY OF MY MOTHER

Table of Contents

Prologue

I grew up in the 1950s in Harrisburg, Pennsylvania, the firstborn child of Margaret "Marg" and Frank "Nick" Nicholson. My dad served stateside in Philadelphia and also somewhere in Oregon as a medic during World War II. He was deferred from going overseas because of a minor physical problem—something about his ears. After the war, my parents bought a house six miles east of the city, more country than suburbia. My two younger sisters and I could walk to school if we didn't feel like waiting for the bus.

As the years passed, Lower Paxton School, a three-story brick building, serving first to twelfth grades, could not contain all the children. Schools began shooting up everywhere. Riding the bus was no longer a choice, but there remained only one high school in Dauphin County until just before I graduated in 1961. I lived in the same small white house with my family until I married at eighteen. Ronda and Diane, my sisters, got to live in the new house, a pink-brick rancher that my parents built—across the street from our old home.

Eventually all three of us left Harrisburg, but we often returned to our parents' home. Whether for a quick weekend visit or an extended stay, there was comfort in the familiar surroundings. I made it home for all but one of our every five-year high school reunions. After the fiftieth, the interval

Peggy, Mom, Daddy, Ronda, Diane
Pink-brick House
1962

MY CHILDHOOD FAMILY TREE

Frank "Nick" Nicholson   Margaret "Marg" Martin
Oct 1920–Sep 1986   Mar 1920–Feb 2003

Margaret "Peggy"   Ronda   Diane

Central Dauphin High School 50th Reunion
Dauphin County 2011

Mom & Daddy
Atlantic City
1984

was shortened to two years, and a picnic replaced the traditional dinner dance.

Though my parents didn't always get along, they stayed married "until death do us part." Daddy died a month before his sixty-sixth birthday. I returned from living abroad in 1996 and bought the house next door to my mother, making it possible for her to live independently until she died in her sleep, not quite eighty-four years old.

The birth of my first and only grandchild, along with the promise of warmer weather, beckoned me to St. Augustine, Florida. In summer 2003, I moved into my new home, an eight minute drive from my daughter, son-in-law, and six-month-old Noah.

My parents were, and always will be, Mom and Daddy to my sisters and me. In my story I often refer to them

as Marg and Nick, especially when talking about their lives before I was born. In family trees, I refer to myself as Peggy, my lifelong nickname.

Noah & Oma (Peggy)
St Augustine
August 2003
60th birthday

My Surprise Family

PART I Cousins

Contents

1

Jumping on the DNA Bandwagon

Years ago, the expense of a DNA test was prohibitive for idle curiosity. Now, genetic tests are affordable and people sometimes do them only to see an estimate of where their ancestors from thousands of years ago lived. Getting tested in a laboratory required a lot of effort, from finding a lab to making an appointment. Now, ordering a DNA kit is as convenient as buying a book on Amazon.com. Previously, people were subjected to a blood-drawing needle. Now, only a cheek swab or a little tube for spit is required. All together, these changes resulted in huge commercial databases permitting people to compare their DNA to others'. It's not surprising that millions of people are jumping on the bandwagon. But would I have jumped if not for Susan Martin?

Susan, my mother's half sister (same dad, different mothers), set everything in motion by forwarding an email from Ancestry.com announcing a sale on DNA kits for the upcoming Thanksgiving weekend. The message arrived late at night, just before I turned off my computer.

I had compared DNA-testing companies, and for my purposes, decided Ancestry.

com would be the best choice. But I was dragging my feet. If I were to forge ahead, I wanted my sisters to get tested too. Without being able to compare my DNA to theirs, I (mistakenly) thought my results would be meaningless.

When I awoke the next morning, my ambivalence was gone. I forwarded the sale announcement to each sister with a quick note.

Date: November 22, 2016
Subject: DNA Sale
Ronda & Diane,
Now's your chance to get your DNA tested! I'm going to do it. I think you should too. Let's see if we have the same father. ha! ha!
Peggy

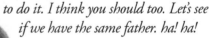

More than a decade ago, at my mother's memorial service, Jae, a long-time friend, said she believed I had a different father because I was so unlike my sisters with my ambitious personality and optimistic attitude. Proving her idea

Jae and Peggy
March 2003

wrong played a role in my interest in getting tested. Growing up, there was neither an indication from Mom and Dad nor a thought in my mind that such a thing could be true. I even had my own conception story about Daddy home on furlough during World War II.

I registered for an Ancestry.com guest account and ordered my DNA kit. To my surprise, I felt just like I do after buying a plane ticket to visit a country overseas—an adventure was waiting for me.

Both my sisters joined me on the bandwagon, which surprised me, given the expense. We received our kits within days of each other, but the delay in returning them seemed to follow our birth order. I am the oldest, and it took me about two weeks to get around to reading and following through on the instructions. The small kit box had gotten "lost" for a few days among my usual mess of books on the couch or papers on my desk. Ronda, younger by two and a half years, delayed for a month. Diane, four and a half years younger than me, waited even longer to send in her kit.

I was looking forward to having fun with the DNA results when they arrived. The genealogical aspect—tracing my family back to the countries from which my ancestors came—truly interested me. Maybe I could even find DNA relatives who still lived in the Old World.

2

Who's Ashley?

Five weeks after filling a little tube with spit and returning it to Ancestry.com, the laboratory finished comparing my genetic material to others who had returned their kits. I had 389 4th cousins or closer. I clicked the link to see who these people were, these genetic relatives. The top three were labeled as 1st cousins. I recognized the first name as belonging to Susan, the second was Ashley_rn28, and the third was Susan's daughter Beth. Who's Ashley?

There were two people under the 2nd cousin heading and ten listed as 3rd cousins. The last category, 4th or closer cousins, went on and on. I had no interest in these hundreds of others because my attention was focused on this Ashley person. I knew all my first cousins, eleven on my paternal Nicholson side and three on my maternal Martin side. We had grown up together—there was no Ashley among them.

~ MEMORY ~

Thinking about my cousins brought back vivid memories from my childhood. My grandparents, on both sides, had lived in the Greater Harrisburg area, and their children remained in the area as they raised their children. We cousins saw each other often at birthday parties and holidays. For a while, even the grownups had birthday parties at which gifts brought gales of laughter. We kids could participate in the laughter at times—Uncle Hen unwrapped a ratty-looking toupee and plunked it on his bald head. Other times, we didn't get the joke and weren't allowed to look too closely at the gifts.

In the summer, cousins took turns sleeping at each other's houses. We easily adapted our behavior to each aunt's expectations—from one with many, clear rules to the others with fewer, but inconsistent, rules. You could do almost anything at Aunt Betty's except roller-skate on Sundays. Aunt Marg, my mother, was the favorite—"Do whatever you want!"

My mother's behavior at home when no one else was around sometimes differed from how she was with others—like night and day—more like a nightmare and a bright sunshiny day. In my mid-forties, after a counselor convinced me parents are neither all good nor all bad, I finally stopped flip-flopping between "My mother was wonderful because …," and "My mother was horrible because …."

When we were very young, and our grandparents and their siblings—our great-aunts and great-uncles—were still alive, there were summer reunions. First, second, and third cousins played together, though no one knew the relationships as such. They were just relatives, family—that's all we needed to know.

Eventually, as the older generations disappeared and *we* became the parents, cousins began dispersing. Some remained in Pennsylvania, but moved more than fifty miles from Harrisburg—to Pittsburgh and Philadelphia. I went off to Philly with a second husband—too far away for a casual afternoon birthday party. Others went out of state to North Carolina, Connecticut, Iowa, and even off the "mainland." After Ronda moved to Hawaii, if we slipped and asked, "When are you coming to the US?" her indignant response would be, "You mean the mainland?"

Later, I left the country altogether and lived in the Netherlands for six years. When I moved back to the US, instead of returning to Philadelphia, I bought a house next door to my mother on the street where I had grown up. Once again, I was close enough to participate in holiday parties with relatives in the Harrisburg area.

When Uncle Hen got his gag-gift toupee, I was about ten years old. When I was sixty, cousin Jayne invited everyone to her house for Christmas dinner. This was the last Christmas we had with my mother. Jayne bought gag gifts for everyone. I still wear mine to sleep in—an oversized T-shirt printed with the words: "HELP! I'm talking and I can't shut up."

～ ～ ～ ～

Thinking about the past wouldn't help me figure out who Ashley was. I phoned and emailed cousins, trying to find out if their children or grandchildren had their DNA tested. I asked everyone, "Is anyone named Ashley?" Cousin Jayne tried to be helpful: "Anne Marie used to have a dog named Ashley." I called Anne Marie in Connecticut. She prefers Anne, but we who grew up with her can't get used to it. Once she told me colleagues at her workplace would say, "Someone's on the phone asking for Anne Marie, it must be for you." She knew that meant a relative was calling and wondered who was sick or dead. When I reached her, Anne Marie said neither she nor her daughters were tested: "No, I don't know anyone in the family named Ashley."

I couldn't even be sure the person behind the display name was called Ashley. My sisters and I, along with many others, chose to display our real names—first and last. Others made up display names, such as "treegayzer" and "meryer2121." Many simply used two initials. Maybe Ashley *was* the name of a dog, just not Anne Marie's.

It was nerve wracking thinking there was a first

**Martin First Cousins
Allen, Scott, Ross
~1953**

**Nicholson First Cousins
~1957**

cousin I didn't know about. Then I got a call from Susan: "You and Ashley share a lot of DNA. It's more than the average amount of centiMorgans for a first cousin." I had no idea what she was talking about, but the urgency in her voice was enough to send a shiver down my back. I did know "centi" was a unit of measurement meaning one-hundredth. I found a variety of DNA charts online and some complicated explanations about what was being measured by a centiMorgan. To understand the charts would require more concentration than I had at the moment. I'd confront that task later. For the time being, I was content knowing centiMorgans, abbreviated as cMs, represented the amount of shared gene segments between two people or, even easier for me to remember, the amount of shared DNA.

I was thinking of Ashley as "she" because the circle next to her name was pink, which meant female was chosen for the DNA Profile. As usual, blue was used for males. Many people upload a photo of themselves to the circle. Someone with a sense of humor posted a picture of a cat. The best way to find out about this Ashley person was to use Ancestry.com's internal messaging feature. To appear open and receptive, I included my telephone number.

Date: December 28, 2016

Subject: How are we related?

Ashley

I just got these DNA results—have no idea how this works. I am from Harrisburg, PA. Mom's birth name was Margaret Martin, her mom was a Briner. Dad is Frank Nicholson.

Peggy

Tel: 111 111-1111

I waited for a reply, hoping it wouldn't be long.

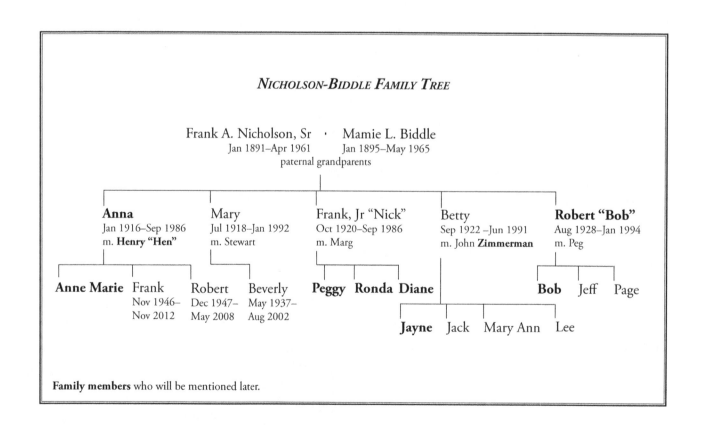

NICHOLSON-BIDDLE FAMILY TREE

Frank A. Nicholson, Sr   ·   Mamie L. Biddle
Jan 1891–Apr 1961   Jan 1895–May 1965
                paternal grandparents

Anna   Mary   Frank, Jr "Nick"   Betty   **Robert "Bob"**
Jan 1916–Sep 1986   Jul 1918–Jan 1992 Oct 1920–Sep 1986   Sep 1922–Jun 1991   Aug 1928–Jan 1994
m. **Henry "Hen"**   m. Stewart   m. Marg   m. John **Zimmerman**   m. Peg

Anne Marie Frank   Robert   Beverly   **Peggy** **Ronda** Diane   **Bob**   Jeff   Page
               Nov 1946–   Dec 1947–   May 1937–
               Nov 2012   May 2008   Aug 2002

                                                                       Jayne Jack Mary Ann Lee

Family members who will be mentioned later.

3

How Are We Related?

As I suspected, after I registered for the free account, then bought and activated my test kit, I became totally absorbed in adding relatives to my family tree. When my DNA results appeared, I began spending long hours late into the night looking through genetic matches, sending pleading-type messages: "Please look at my family tree and tell me how we are related?" My first message to Ashley was minimal and mentioned both sides of my family. I expected an immediate answer, but five days passed…slowly…very slowly…without an answer from her.

In the meantime, Susan, my personal "help manual," explained why Ashley and I couldn't be related through Irvin Martin's—her father, my maternal grandfather—family line. She was not among the DNA matches I shared with Ashley. This meant the DNA Ashley and I shared had to come from a different genetic ancestor.

Irvin Martin is Susan's and my most

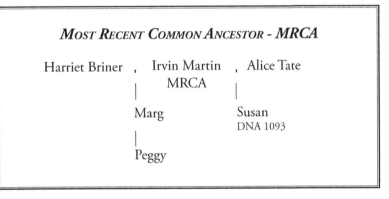

MOST RECENT COMMON ANCESTOR - MRCA

Harriet Briner , Irvin Martin , Alice Tate
                        MRCA

Marg   Susan
                            DNA 1093

Peggy

Harriet & Irvin
with Marg & Doris
~1924

recent common ancestor, abbreviated as MRCA. Susan and my mother inherited genes directly from their father. The genes I share with Susan came to me from my grandfather through my mother. These probably aren't the words a scientist would use, but ordinary language helped me understand and more quickly identify common or shared ancestors.

When it comes to kinship patterns on the Martin line, Susan, as my mother's sister, is a generation "above" me. Though close in age—she is four years younger—one of us will always be "once removed" in relation to mutual cousins.

Because Susan and Mom had different mothers, there was still a chance Ashley and I were related through my maternal grandmother, Harriet Briner (Nana). Doris, my mother's full sister, had three sons. I checked and was disappointed to learn neither they nor their children had sent in test kits.

All was not lost. My grandmother's maiden name was Briner, and I had two DNA matches who appeared to be Briners. "Brinernut" was listed in the 2nd cousin category, the other, L.B., in the 3rd. Brinernut managed L.B.'s account. Both had DNA linked to the same tree of 12,338 people. I hadn't yet paid for a subscription to see family trees, but I assumed they were my grandmother's Briners. Because

they were close, not distant, cousins, exactly how we were related didn't matter for the time being. (See Briner Cousins Revealed)

I searched through my shared matches with each of them. Since everyone—except identical twins—inherit different genes from parents, who shows up in a list of shared matches will vary, even among siblings. But this is more likely to be the case for distant cousins. Ashley was nowhere to be seen among the Briners' shared matches with me. Ashley did not belong on my maternal grandmother's side of the family either.

Triangulating with shared matches to identify relatives was new to me, but with this evidence I felt forced to acknowledge that Ashley was on the paternal side of my family. If the amounts of DNA involved weren't so high, I would have hesitated to rule out my maternal side. But Ashley's and Susan's close genetic match to me, along with the two Briner cousins, allowed little room for error.

Another question remained to be answered: Did Ashley belong in my Nicholson tree or did I belong in her family tree—a family I didn't know. Was she a Nicholson or was I the one with the wrong surname?

I had to take a break from "Ashley," which to me

MATERNAL GRANDPARENTS

Harriet Briner · Irvin Martin
May 1893–May 1987   Mar 1893–Dec 1948

Marg   Doris

Peggy   Ronda   Diane   Allen   Ross   Scott

Irvin & Harriet
with Marg & Doris
~1938

Briner Family 1916-17
Sara, Gertrude (mother),
Dewey, Garb, Edward
(father), Floyd, Aunt Maggie
(Edward's sister), taken by
Harriet

Briner Family 1938
Sara, Hope, Floyd,
Garb, Edward &
Gertrude, (parents)
Harriet (my
grandma), Dewey

no longer referred to a DNA match or even to a specific person. The name had come to represent a goal or a concept—both exciting and terrifying at the same time—like a ride on a huge roller coaster. Except when a roller coaster ride is over and the bar unlocks, I step out of the car, back onto solid ground, and nothing has changed.

How did I slip from my fun journey into genealogy and end up agonizing over genes?

BRINER-GARBER GREAT-GRANDPARENTS

Edward G. Briner   ·   Gertrude J. Garber
Apr 1869–Aug 1949   Mar 1869–June 1941

Harriet	A. Hope	Sara G.	R. Dewey	C. Garber	E. Floyd
May 1893–	Sep 1894–	Jan 1896–	Dec 1897–	Mar 1902–	Sep 1904–
May 1987	Jan 1970	Dec 1982	Apr 1979	Sep 2000	Jan 1965
m. Irvin Martin	m. David Elder	m. Paul Shreffler	m. Esther	m. Helen	m. Effie

Marg Doris   Edward   Emmett Virginia "Sis" Bill   Edward "Moe" Bill   Shirley Bob   Lee   Dick Dale

Briner Cousins Revealed

After paying for a Subscription, I was surprised to see, according to the Briner tree, that the cousins were sisters. L.B. shared 361 centiMorgans (cMs) with me and was listed in the 2nd cousin category, while Brinernut, listed as a 3rd cousin, shared 153 cMs. With fewer cMs, I expected to see her in the tree as a daughter to L.B.

The range of cMs for a second cousin is 46–515 with an expected average of 233, and for a third cousin, the range is 0–217 with an expected average of 74. With the overlap in the amount of cMs caused by the wide range, it made perfect sense that both Briners could be second cousins. (See ISOGG.org for more details and DNA charts.)

I knew immediately how we were related when I saw the name of their grandfather, Clyde Garber Briner. Uncle Garb was Nana's brother. I was probably around him when I was a small child, before he moved to Florida. Assuming the DNA for each cousin was attached to the correct person in the tree, our MRCAs were our great-grandparents Gertrude and Edward Briner. The Briners are a good reminder that the kinship categories on the Website are not meant to designate exact relationships.

I tried for months to reach Brinernut to say hello and get the cousins' names for my tree, but she never answered my messages. One day I noticed something didn't make sense between the Briners' accounts and their tree. In my list of matches, L.B.

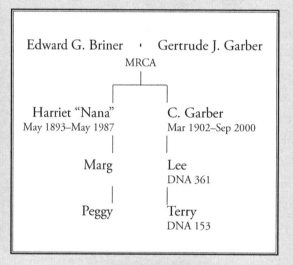

Edward G. Briner · Gertrude J. Garber
MRCA

Harriet "Nana"
May 1893–May 1987

C. Garber
Mar 1902–Sep 2000

Marg

Lee
DNA 361

Peggy

Terry
DNA 153

had a blue circle—the DNA was registered as belonging to a male, but when I clicked to see "him" in the tree, the person in the tree was pink, a "she."

I thought L.B. might be Garb's son, Lee. To make a long story short, I did an online search using "obituary Lee Garber." He had recently passed away making his obituary easily accessible. Using the unusual name of one of his grandchildren, I was able to locate the family. Brinernut turned out to be my second cousin, Terry, Lee's son. We figured out that she had mistakenly attached her father's DNA to her name in the tree. I directed her to Settings, and, as we spoke by phone, she got her father's DNA attached to his own name.

After Lee's DNA was in the right spot, Terry and I went on to talk for more than an hour. Garb had moved his family to Venice, Florida, and started a motel. I think it was the first one in Florida. Eventually they moved to the mid-west.

Our conversation reminded me of a trip my parents took to Florida when my sisters and I were little and stayed home with relatives. I have snapshots of Mom & Dad with people I don't recognize. Surely Mom wouldn't have traveled from Pennsylvania to Florida and not visit her first cousin. That may have been the reason for the trip. I told Terry I would scan and post the photos. As a child, my vision of Florida was of brightly painted gourds—a souvenir that hung on the back of our kitchen door. The gourds are back in Florida, hanging from my kitchen ceiling.

4

Jetting Off into Genealogy with Noah

To stop thinking about my genetic relationship with Ashley for a while, I returned to traditional genealogy, non-DNA style, and focused on building my family tree. I had a vague idea that genealogy, the study of family ancestral lines, was named after genes—those small sections of DNA in our bodies that code for proteins. But I had it backward. According to Genome.gov, a website that has more content than anyone would have time to read in a lifetime, Wilhelm Johannsen coined the term "genes" as recently as 1908. Genealogy, on the other hand, has been around centuries, but my interest began during a summer trip with my grandson Noah.

~ MEMORY ~

In June 2012, I took my nine-year-old grandson Noah to Harrisburg. I wanted him to get to know his relatives, the family members I had grown up with. I was also eager to show him the Capitol building and the Pennsylvania State Museum, places I had taken my children when they were his age. Would the peephole still be there so children could see, without standing on a stool, the underwater view of a dam built by beavers? I remember how much my sisters and I liked these dioramas: animals, preserved by a taxidermist, appeared alive in their own habitats. How will they not look bedraggled and moth-eaten if they are the same beavers my children enjoyed over forty-five years ago?

Mom-mom & Noah Jan 2003

Our relatives had met Noah as an infant, when my daughter Sherry, had taken him to meet his great-grandmother, my mother, who lived next door to me. "Mom-mom" died a month after she held her great-grandson. I love the photograph of her holding him, both of them looking directly into the camera.

On this trip, closer to ten years old than nine, Noah seemed old enough to me to grasp how everyone was related. I wanted him to understand whether we were spending time with the Nicholson family on my dad's side or the Martin family on my mom's side. I also wanted him to know how he was related to each cousin, their children and grandchildren. This meant explaining who my parents' siblings were so he could associate the names of my aunts and uncles with the right cousin. Of course, he wouldn't get to meet that generation—everyone but Aunt Doris was dead.

Cousin Jayne, as she generously did whenever I came to town, invited the Nicholson crowd to a potluck at her house. She and her son are both great cooks. The macaroni and cheese are the best I've ever eaten.

There were thirty or so people milling around between the kitchen and the patio, eating and talking. We couldn't remember from one get-together to the next what the kinship term was for us to the others' children or our children to each other. Add grandchildren and we were completely lost. But for this visit I studied a chart ahead of time and had come prepared with the knowledge securely in mind.

To get Noah's attention as he passed my chair, I grabbed his hand, pointed to the people around us, and, without giving it a second thought, included dead relatives in my genealogical explanation.

That's Dawn, your second cousin once removed. There's Dawn's mom, Cousin Jayne. Jayne's mom and dad were Aunt Betty and Uncle John Zimmerman who owned the coffee and candy shop we went to yesterday. Aunt Betty was my daddy's sister—your great-grandpa Pop-pop who died before you were born.

Noah tolerated my long-winded description until he could pull free. He was eager to get back to the game he was playing with Dawn's son Cole. As he ran off I hollered after him:

"Cole is your third cousin!"

How ridiculous that any of this would make sense, let alone be meaningful to Noah. But it meant something to me. The people at the picnic and the ones long gone and buried remained an important part of my life. I was sad that in contrast to how my sisters and I grew up, surrounded by extended family, Noah's relatives were scattered far and wide.

The food was put away, but no one seemed ready to leave. I got out a card game I had brought along. No one had heard of it, but everyone was eager to participate. We played into the evening until the Nicholsons who had come the farthest got up to go.

We were on our way to Manheim, a forty-minute drive southeast of Harrisburg, My cousin Allen and his wife Judy invited the Martins to their home, a re-done, old farm house with a barn beside it. Judy always took care of all the food. I thought of her as the hostess-with-the-mostest.

I had hopes that Noah could master the genealogy on the Martin side because Mom grew up with one sister (not four siblings like Daddy), and Aunt Doris had only three sons. I reminded Noah, "We're going to see your great-great-aunt Doris." I wanted him to associate her loving warmth toward him with my mother. "She's my mother's sister. Remember Mom-mom? You have a picture of her holding you as a little baby. It's in your bedroom on the chiffarobe."

When we arrived, Aunt Doris, at eighty-nine, was still lively and as much fun to be around as always. It was hard to get Noah's attention for my genealogy lesson. My cousin Allen, with his foot hovering near the brake, was letting Noah and his grandchildren take turns driving a golf cart up and down the hills in the backyard, hills higher than on our Florida roads.

Susan, whom I didn't know very well, didn't always make it to our get-togethers, so the rest of us were glad to see her. She's the only one of Irvin Martin's descendants who carries the Martin name. (I added Martin as my middle name when I reverted from a married name back to Nicholson.) We sat talking at the picnic table, as the golf cart careened around the yard. I was telling everyone that being with Noah around family made me want to get everyone's names and birth dates written down. The number of generations below me was increasing, and I didn't know all the names of my cousins' grandchildren.

Susan jumped in and suggested I build a family tree online: "Sign up for a guest account, and then I'll invite you by email to see my Martin tree." She insisted that having an account and viewing her tree would not cost anything.

I was more than willing to exchange emails to share names and dates of family members, but I was resistant to signing up for a "free" account. Free financially doesn't mean free when it comes to time. Besides, Ancestry.com would certainly send me emails enticing me with offers of additional services.

On the flight home, I asked Noah to name three things he liked most about our trip. They were on the tip of his tongue: Getting lots of candy at Zimmerman's in Penbrook, driving the golf cart at the picnic with Aunt Doris, and looking for snakes in the mammal dioramas at the museum.

I loved every single minute of the trip and didn't want to pick favorites, but playing Five Crowns with the Nicholson crowd was special because of the memories it brought back. I told Noah about how the adults used to play penny ante poker when our families got together. I would sit on Uncle Bob's lap, stacking the pennies he won. We cousins hadn't carried on the card playing tradition, so that day at Jayne's was so much fun, especially with the children playing too. Everyone was laughing and teasing … just like old times.

~ ~ ~ ~

After my trip to Harrisburg, I had collected genealogical information from both sides of my family. My cousins responded to my emails and had given me the birth, marriage,

**Noah with
Great-great-aunt Doris
Manheim
June 2012**

and death dates of their parents. I began transferring the information to my online tree. Every so often, after adding five or six names and dates, I would pause to refresh my screen, hoping a little number would appear on the message envelope letting me know someone had answered one of my "How are we related?" inquiries. But no such luck. I filled my tree with all my grandparents, aunts and uncles, and cousins. Playing around with the tree distracted me for a while, but thoughts of DNA matches ruined my concentration.

Mastering Second Cousins & Cousins Once Removed

At a family get-together with the Nicholsons, my dad's side of the family, we got into the "how is everyone related" discussion again. There's never a question about first cousins. Why are all the other cousin categories so confusing? Perhaps I should have thought of bringing a nice big chart with everyone's name and relationship, but I hadn't.

When "doing ancestry" (regardless of which company you are using), it's impossible not to confront the cousin situation if you want to identify how you are related to people in your family tree or your DNA matches. I had come to understand the cousin terminology, but couldn't always make it clear to others.

There are numerous online charts, but it's much more satisfying to truly understand what these relationships mean. It's all about your grandparents at different levels: great, second-great, third-great and so on. Add in their children, who are siblings to each other, and except for your parent, they are your aunts and uncles, again at different levels.

First, use your intuitive understanding of first cousins as the building block for cousins at the second, third, and so forth levels. First cousins have the same grandparents and call each other's parents, aunt and uncle. The children of first cousins are second cousins to each other, the children of second cousins are third cousins to each other, and so forth down the line. This means the grandparent of a first cousin is the great-grandparent of a second cousin, and the aunts and uncles of first cousins are great-aunts and great-uncles to second cousins.

The "removed" part usually trips people up, but if you think or say to yourself, "How many generations am I removed, that is, *away* from my first (second, third, etc.) cousin?" My first cousin's child is one generation away from or removed from me. My first cousin Jayne's daughter, Dawn, is my first cousin once removed (from Jayne). Dawn's son is my first cousin twice removed (from Jayne).

Don't forget that generations move "up" as well as "down." Your parent's first cousins are also your first cousins once removed (from you)!

Something else to keep in mind when discussing relationships—a point so obvious I feel silly pointing it out. Kinship designations vary depending upon the reference. After telling my grandson Noah, "My grandmother gave *me* this toy at the same age *you* are now," I paused. Then, thinking it important to describe her relationship to him, added, "She is your great-great-grandmother." Of course, he understood the first sentence, but once the words "your great-great-grandmother" left my mouth, the symbolism of the moment was ruined.

A better example of my point and its relevance to cousins once removed is the situation with Susan and me. In our relationship to Irvin Martin, Susan is his daughter, while I'm his granddaughter. I'm older than Susan, but age is irrelevant when it comes to generational kinships. Cousins on the Martin side are "once more removed" for either one of us.

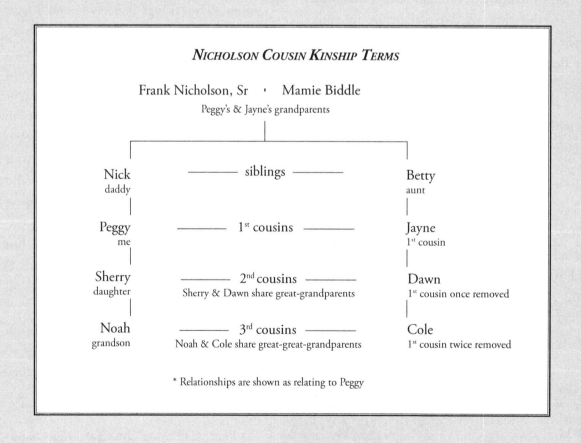

NICHOLSON COUSIN KINSHIP TERMS

Frank Nicholson, Sr · Mamie Biddle
Peggy's & Jayne's grandparents

Nick daddy	—— siblings ——	Betty aunt
Peggy me	—— 1st cousins ——	Jayne 1st cousin
Sherry daughter	—— 2nd cousins —— Sherry & Dawn share great-grandparents	Dawn 1st cousin once removed
Noah grandson	—— 3rd cousins —— Noah & Cole share great-great-grandparents	Cole 1st cousin twice removed

* Relationships are shown as relating to Peggy

5

My Other 50 Percent

Not thinking about my mystery-match Ashley for a few hours did me a world of good. Now that I was convinced Ashley didn't belong on the maternal side of my family, I turned my attention to my other half, the paternal side.

Susan, experienced in identifying DNA matches, tried to be helpful by creating a family tree that accommodated both Ashley and me.

Date: January 15, 2017

Subject: Ashley-Peggy tree

Hi

Any progress on Ashley? I need to see things visually, so I constructed a partial tree showing all of the grandparents including yours, with Nick as your father and also with an unknown male as a father. The other possibility would be if she is a descendant of one of Irv's brothers or sisters.

I am attaching it but my thought process might be hard for someone else to follow.

Susan

Susan's tree made me uncomfortable. Why push the idea on me of a probable different father? She was right that I might have difficulty following her thinking. In one part I was connected by a line to my dad "Nick," but was also listed a second time under "Unknown Male." Looking at that line made my skin crawl. Besides, wasn't it more likely that my father, not my mother, had an inappropriate liaison? Her chart showed this option too. My father and his four siblings were in a box to show Ashley could have been a descendant of any of the five. Trying to sort through all these possibilities would turn out to be a big waste of time, when, as I suspected (hoped?), Ashley showed up in my sister's DNA results.

So why did the uneasiness continue? There were pages and pages of people I was related to who shared DNA with Ashley and me. These were different from those on my maternal side. That made sense—I had to have paternal relatives—the other 50 percent of my genes. What bothered me, made me itchy, was that the names were completely

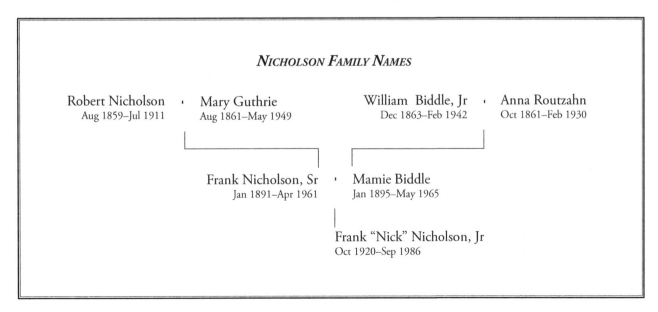

Nicholson Family Names

| Robert Nicholson | · | Mary Guthrie | | William Biddle, Jr | · | Anna Routzahn |
| Aug 1859–Jul 1911 | | Aug 1861–May 1949 | | Dec 1863–Feb 1942 | | Oct 1861–Feb 1930 |

Frank Nicholson, Sr · Mamie Biddle
Jan 1891–Apr 1961   Jan 1895–May 1965

Frank "Nick" Nicholson, Jr
Oct 1920–Sep 1986

unfamiliar to me. I tried taking comfort in the fact that many people preferred creating a name for display purposes for confidentiality. But none of these contained familiar parts as I had found among my maternal matches, such as Brinernut.

There was not one Nicholson, neither a Biddle, my grandma's maiden name, nor a Guthrie, my great-grandmother's maiden name. Growing up, I knew those names. We joked around, saying, "Grandma, are you sure you aren't related to the rich Biddles in Philadelphia?" I think she was, just not close enough to inherit money. Perhaps I will happen onto a Philadelphia Biddle as I add to her branch of my tree.

From building my tree, I learned more names. Grandma's mother was a Routzahn or Routzong. Early on, I had to resign myself to being open-minded about the spelling of names. This was especially true if the name pronounced in the immigrant's native tongue could only be replicated with American-spelled syllables.

I wasn't giving up and thought that with specific information, Ashley would at least respond, if only to write, "I don't know those names—they aren't my family."

Date: December 27, 2016

Subject: Nicholson update

Dear Ashley,

I think you must be related on my father's side: Nicholson. My grandmother was a Biddle, my grandfather was Frank Nicholson. His mother was a Guthrie. My other great-grandmother was a Routzong or Routzahn. They lived in Gettysburg before moving to Harrisburg.

I'd love to hear from you.

Peggy

Three weeks went by. I kept busy building my tree on both the Martin and the Nicholson sides. While I don't give up easily, I got a bit testy in my next message.

Date: January 17, 2017

Subject: Cousins

Hi,

You come up as a first cousin. Will you let me know who you are?

Peggy

These weren't very friendly messages, and I wouldn't blame anyone who had read them for not responding. On the other hand, perhaps Ashley hadn't seen them. I checked her DNA profile page and saw she hadn't signed in for almost four months. Then again, the contents of messages are embedded in the email alerts account holders receive. Was she reading my messages and ignoring them, or had she blocked Ancestry.com from sending emails?

I prefer email and stay away from mobile texting and Facebook messaging, but many people check email less frequently, relying instead on texting. Ashley is young. I liked to think she hadn't seen my messages yet, rather than simply ignoring them.

Perhaps one of our shared matches could tell me who Ashley was. I sent messages to a few people, asking for help.

Date: January 20, 2017

Subject: Our relationship?

Hi,

Just had my DNA done. Do you know how we are related? Also, you come up as shared match to someone who is listed as my 1st cousin (Ashley_rn28).

Because I should know all my first cousins, this seems exciting. I've written to Ashley, but haven't heard back as yet.

Perhaps you know who she is?

Peggy

The few who answered seemed willing to help, but had no idea how we were related to each other or who Ashley was. What a waste of time! Why was I going to all this trouble seeking a familiar name among our shared matches and taking time to write message after message? Why was I ignoring the obvious way to learn more about her.

The day my DNA results arrived, I saw that Ashley's tree included 144 people. Because the number of people was visible to me, I knew she linked her DNA to her tree. Since Ashley and I shared a significant amount of centiMorgans, I thought it likely I might recognize how we were related by looking in her tree. Why didn't I open it and look?

Viewing trees requires a subscription. Ancestry.com had been sending tantalizing discount offers. My conscious reason for delaying the purchase was to avoid paying longer than necessary. My plan was to limit myself to one six-month subscription which should be sufficient to find the ancestors who emigrated from the Old World.

Lack of money was not the issue. I'm not cheap, just frugal. (For years, with a phone call I renewed *The New Yorker* for an academic rate of $25.)

I would buy a subscription as soon as my sister Ronda's DNA results arrived. If Ashley appeared in her list of matches, which I assumed would happen, the mystery of Ashley's identity might not be solved, but at least there would be proof I didn't have a different father.

I wished I felt as sure as I sounded.

6

All About Susan

I didn't want to think about what I'd do if I never heard from Ashley. I teased Susan. "It's all your fault I'm in this DNA pickle." I wasn't mad at her. We were having a lot of fun, not only with the Ashley mystery, but working on the Martin genealogy too. We were getting to know each other.

The Martin get-together in 2012 may have been the first time since my mother's funeral nine years earlier that we saw each other. Without that quick exchange of email addresses at the picnic table, I doubt my DNA would have made it into any company's database. For the first few years, we sporadically exchanged emails about our Martin genealogy. Susan had been focused on her mother's family history, tracing ancestors to the 1500s in England and the 1600s in Scotland. She was eager to turn her attention to Irvin Martin—her father, my grandfather—and was glad to have me as a co-researcher.

Susan left, on Irvin's knee, Alice in short dress, Marg 4th from left, Peggy right standing, Ronda front center

I wanted to know where the Martins came from but was more curious about my other three grandparents whom I knew well. Grandpa Martin died when I was only five. The funny thing was the only time I remembered seeing him was when he came to our house with Susan.

~ *MEMORY* ~

The first time I saw Susan, she was a small baby in the arms of my grandfather, Irvin Martin. This would have happened late in 1947. Perhaps it was a Christmas visit. I remember them standing just inside the front door of our little Cape Cod–style house. I believe it is a true memory because there is no photograph of it. I was around Grandpa other times—there are pictures, but no memories to go along with them. I do like looking at the one of my cousin Allen and me wearing swimsuits in a rowboat. Grandpa died the following December, the day after Christmas. I wonder if he got to see Susan take her first steps.

The day of their visit, someone sat me in the corner of the sofa and put a pillow on my lap so I could hold Susan. This may have been the moment that sparked my desire to hold every baby I got near and made me eager to have one of my own.

At that age, I wouldn't have understood Grandpa was also my mother's father or known he and my grandmother Nana had once been married. Eventually I came to know the whole story: She divorced Irvin soon after their two daughters were grown and married: "I told you I would divorce you once my girls could take care of themselves." I can hear Nana's voice because she told me about that early episode and many others. I still have the cassette tapes from 1973 when I recorded her telling me the story of her life for a college project. Irvin then married Alice who, according to Nana, was the reason for the divorce in the first place.

Peggy & Allen with
Grandpa Martin

I wonder what it was like for my mother to greet her baby sister, Susan, when she was pregnant with her own third child. Mom may have originally been upset about the divorce, but certainly not for long since I remember her taking my sisters and me to see Alice and Susan on holidays. They lived only about twenty minutes away. I must have been fairly young when we stopped going.

Though she never spoke to Alice after the divorce, Nana seemed to know so much about the personal life of Irvin and Alice. Nana told me, "Alice was shocked when she found herself in that way." Alice didn't think it was possible to become pregnant because it hadn't happened during her first marriage and now she was even older.

~ ~ ~ ~

One evening not long ago, Susan and I were comparing stories—I was telling her about Nana's gossip and she was sharing some of Alice's thoughts on the situation: "My mother's periods had stopped, but she was afraid to go to the doctor right away because she was sure the bulge in her belly was a tumor. Finally, she went and the doctor examined her. When the doctor said, 'The baby's heartbeat is normal,' my mother fainted."

I brought up the subject of our family visits, which are mostly vague memories. Susan must have remembered the one that stands out in my mind because both involved baskets: "I'll never forget how special I felt when all of you came to visit and brought me an Easter basket."

Today's Susan reminds me of my mom, with her blue eyes and dark hair (at this age, we both admit to using hair color), her height, and energetic, talkative manner. Susan shares the good parts of my mother's personality:

Marg, Susan, Doris ~1998

intellectual curiosity and an accepting attitude toward all kinds of people. When Mom was still alive, anyone seeing them together would assume they were sisters, or because of the twenty-seven-year age gap, mother and daughter.

Susan and I were derailed from our research into the Martin genealogy by the Ashley mystery. This led to more interaction and openness between us. In one email, Susan wrote: "Thank you for sharing all of this with me. Although your mother was my sister, we didn't grow up together. Working on all of this with you is like having a sister for me."

7

Waiting, Waiting, Waiting . . .

I couldn't stop going through my DNA matches, choosing someone at random, clicking on the shared matches tab, then selecting someone within that group to triangulate even further. The more I understood how the shared matches feature worked—by forming successive groups of people who inherited the same genes from a great- or great-great-grandparent or beyond—the more I wanted to identify and add all these cousins to my tree. Once I gained access to their family trees, I could probably figure out who our common ancestors were.

When I wasn't making cross-check lists of who shared DNA with whom, I was on pins and needles waiting for my sister Ronda's test results to show up. She had received an email from Ancestry.com letting her know the kit was being processed. Every thirty minutes I refreshed my DNA summary to see if her name was there.

My anxiety focused on the amount of DNA this Ashley person and I shared. Unless there

was a mistake in the laboratory, we had to be closely related. But how? I grasped at straws and counted on Susan's expertise when I couldn't contain myself. "If Ashley were related to my son Michael, she would have matched the Martins and the Briners, don't you agree?" As I hit the send button, I knew the answer already. "Yes, of course she would, but she doesn't."

I asked Ronda if she had any concerns about the DNA revealing an alternative father for her. She was positive about her paternity: "I'm my father's child." She did inherit his wavy hair and complexion. Ronda didn't mind expressing her opinion that I wasn't the only one who might have a different father: "Maybe Diane does too." I had no idea why she said that. Growing up, we three were considered tomboys. We played outside most of the time, climbed trees, and got dirty. But Ronda was much more into sports, For that reason she believed and wouldn't stop saying, "Daddy is my father."

Before my DNA results showed up, I never had any doubts about who my father was. I always felt like I belonged. In fact, that is one of the things that irritates some people about me. In comparison to a lot of people I know, I am not uncomfortable going alone to an event, even one where I won't know anyone. I'm not sure if the two things have anything to do with each other—my confidence about my place in the world and my sisters' major complaint about me: "You always think you're right."

Ancestry.com must have been inundated with kits, especially with another sale just before the winter holiday season. A banner ran across the Website, warning that results could take as long as eight or more weeks. One of their customer service representatives—easily accessible by phone—told me they had finally acquired another laboratory.

The only way to make the wait bearable was to find new ways to distract myself. After checking for new matches each morning, I continued copying

Diane, Ronda /book, Peggy ~1953

all the family names and dates from the spreadsheet into my family tree. Except for my grandparents, these were what I thought of as the "forward" generations. Then I went "backwards" and added the siblings of my grandparents and the names of my great-grandparents.

My curiosity (anxiety?) was growing stronger by the day. When would Ronda's results get here?

8

No Ashley!

I refreshed the DNA summary tab more and more often, and if the number of my 4th cousins or closer increased by one, I quickly clicked to see if Ronda's results were there. There had been 311 the night before, now there were 312. I clicked. There was my sister Ronda's name under the heading Close Family. Would Ashley show as a shared match with Ronda and me? I pressed the tab and Susan, the Briner cousins, and others I knew on my mother's side of the family appeared.

Where was Ashley? I looked at every one of the DNA matches I shared with Ronda. Ashley wasn't there—she and Ronda did not share DNA.

I was eager to look at all of Ronda's matches, not just the ones she shared with me. I logged into her account. (To see the other's matches, we had exchanged passwords. Later, we instead shared a link to each other's DNA. Viewing another's DNA from within one's own account has advantages.) There was my name in her Close Family group, as I expected. Her first few DNA matches were the same as mine, the ones I knew from my mother's line. Then a familiar name jumped out— Bob Nicholson. He was listed as her 3rd cousin. Their shared matches didn't include me.

Ronda and I both use Nicholson as a surname, having reverted after discarding an assortment of ex-husbands' names. Uncle Bob (Robert Sr), Daddy's brother, had had two sons and a daughter. One of the boys was named Bob (Robert Jr). I phoned my cousin right away but got only his answering machine.

From within Ronda's account, I sent the DNA Bob Nicholson a message, something like, "Are you my cousin Bob whose wife is named … and you live in …?" Would I get a response to my message? If the DNA Bob were my cousin, surely he would answer. But I was pretty sure he wasn't. A month ago when I called around to cousins, hoping to locate "Ashley," Bob's sister told me no one in their family had been tested. Sending the message couldn't hurt.

I was eager to send Susan an email letting her know Ronda's results were here and get her reaction.

Date: January 23, 2017

Subject: No Ashley!

Susan,

Shocking news – Ronda doesn't have Ashley. But she does have a Bob Nicholson as a 3rd cousin who I can't find anywhere in my matches!

Peggy

Once I got the email off to Susan, I turned my attention to Ronda's shared matches with Bob Nicholson. They were completely different from my shared matches with Ashley. Ronda even had a Guthrie!

Up to this point, I resisted looking at the all-important number—the amount of DNA Ronda and I share. A final click on the little *i* and there it was—1853 cMs. The "What does this mean?" chart shows a minimum of 2400 cMs required for full siblings. I remembered hearing that interpreting test results was not always clear cut. Without a parent's DNA to confirm a relationship, siblings could appear to be first cousins or vice versa. Was this still true or was that before DNA testing became more sophisticated?

Could there have been a mistake at the laboratory? Could the *daddy* who raised me not be my *father*?

Measuring Relatedness

The amount of DNA Ashley and I share—1014 centiMorgans—isn't enough for us to be siblings. The expected average for full siblings is 2630, for half siblings 1783. Could she be my dad's granddaughter? I wouldn't be surprised to find he had a child a long time ago. And best of all, there would be no change in my relationship to him.

Studying a relationship chart I downloaded from ISOGG.org, I saw Ashley wasn't likely to be my niece either. I'm disappointed. I find it interesting that the expected average of 1750 for a niece or nephew is about the same as a half sibling. I think of a sibling, even a half, as being closer than the child of one. Then again, the DNA an aunt shares with a niece is from the same two people, one generation removed from aunt to niece. DNA shared with a half sibling comes from only one parent. There is so much to learn.

Then I noticed the amount for a half niece—891 centiMorgans—with a range of 500–1446. Does this mean that Ashley's grandfather could be my biological father?

9

My Daddy

My daddy's friends called him Nick, my younger relatives, Uncle Nick. His brother and sisters called him Junior. After all, when they were growing up, Nick referred to *their* father. My sisters and I never graduated from Daddy to Father.

As an adult, I've written more than a dozen short essays about my mother. The only one I wrote about my daddy was part of an eighth-grade autobiographical assignment with stories and photos. I titled his chapter, "Why I Like My Father." The essay wasn't a complimentary list of reasons for liking him, but an ironic, tongue-in-cheek complaint about his behavior. He worked part-time at a lumberyard on weekends and didn't bring home a piece of wood I needed for a school project.

Another reason I felt neglected was that I almost never got to see him. He worked the three-to-eleven shift on the railroad. He was asleep when I left for school, at work when I got home, and returned home after I had gone to bed. I wrote that he wasn't around enough to remember our names, so referred to my sisters and me as Matilda.

At the end of the chapter, I sweetly justified his behavior as forgetfulness because he was tired from working so much.

During the eighteen years I lived at home, I doubt Daddy and I exchanged more than a paragraph of words. Maybe I'm exaggerating, but not by much. I'm not including the five years before I started kindergarten. Though I don't have specific memories, I imagine he was as wonderfully playful with me when I was a small child as I saw him be with his grandchildren.

Daddy was also sociable and outgoing when a crowd was around—whether it was the Nicholson or the Martin gang getting together. He loved being the host behind the bar in the recreation room of the new house my parents built the year after I left home. The bar was built by my first husband, the father of those grandchildren.

My second marriage took me to Philadelphia. I was learning about family systems in a master's program in psychology. This gave me the idea I could change the dynamics between Daddy and me. I drove to Harrisburg to visit my parents the

Daddy & Peggy sledding ~1946
Little white house in Paxtonia

weekend of his birthday. I wanted one-on-one time. For his birthday, I handed him a nice card that read:

> *Daddy,*
> *I don't know you well enough to choose a present. This card is good for a birthday lunch.*
> *Love, Peggy*

My mother tried to improve on my idea: "He always gets up early but likes to go back to bed to rest or watch TV. Why don't you go for breakfast instead of lunch?"

Saturday morning came and I had to overcome his resistance to leave the house and drive to a restaurant. It was torturous, making conversation as best we could. Quick in, order fast, eat without pause, hurried payment, and straight home.

Early afternoon, I was in the kitchen with Mom as she was making her own breakfast. She never got up before one or two, having gone to bed in the wee hours of the morning because she was busy watching TV and puttering, maybe cleaning the oven or bathroom. "How'd your birthday breakfast go?" she asked.

"Good." My response revealed that I had not set my expectations too high. I did get my alone time with my dad, but assumed that would be the end of our interaction unless I gave him the same present for his next birthday.

The following morning when I dragged myself out of bed and stumbled into the living room, he stood up, heading for the door. "I thought you were never getting up sleepyhead. Let's go. I'm hungry."

Off we went, not as hurried as yesterday and conversation coming a bit easier. The breakfast tradition became a habit and carried over to my sisters, niece, and daughter when they were in town. My daughter, Sherry, told me, "The best fun was when Pop-pop and I got up early and made it out the door before anyone else was awake." She loved having him all to herself.

Eventually we added after-breakfast trips to K-Mart, garage sales, or the trash picker, where clothing was in dumpster-type bins. We had to climb in and walk on the clothes we were picking through. The clothing sold for ten cents a pound. Years after Daddy died, I could turn down an aisle in a K-Mart, and the smell of oil would bring tears to my eyes.

Spending time talking at breakfast carried over to other times we were together, but mostly as chit-chat or joking around. Breakfast was the only time for a real discussion. When I was doing research for my doctoral dissertation, I was telling him about the way the labor unions affect the management of supermarkets. Daddy didn't often express serious opinions, so the few times he did stand out in my mind: "The managers think they know better how to get a job done,"

I enjoyed listening as he talked about his experiences in the railroaders' union and how he and the other workers dealt with managers. The managers wanted to impose their ideas, instead of trusting the men to know the best way to get work done. When that happened, the railroaders would "work to rule"—they'd adhere to the union contract. In contrast to completing the work in less than eight hours and going home early with full pay, finishing the job now required overtime. The company was forced to pay time and half for the extra hours.

When I asked what the managers did, he laughed and said, "They would have to give up and let us do it our way. Then things would go back to normal for a while until some other hotshot college guy showed up and we'd have to teach him a lesson."

I have a video taken by Daddy in 1984 of me changing the oil in my 1974 Dodge Dart. He talks as the camera rolls, saying smart-aleck things and doing a funny riff on asking directions to I-95. A couple of others standing around chimed in. They were all laughing while I struggled. When I put the video in my VCR, I see the car with my legs sticking out from underneath. I can't see him, but the sound of Daddy's voice brings him alive.

He was the cameraman at family functions, so unless someone grabbed the camera when he laid it down, Daddy was rarely filmed. Once someone got a couple minutes of him and Mom dancing. Not a boring slow dance, but the jitterbug. When my parents danced, they always looked happy and never argued. I guess my love for swing dancing came from watching them.

When I had the opportunity to dance with Daddy, I attempted to follow his lead—tried keeping pace with his intricate rhythm and steps. But he wouldn't cut me any slack, and I usually had to give up in frustration. I set a challenge for myself to learn to follow such good dancers. Over the years, in addition to taking dance classes, I used peer counseling with a dance instructor for a few weeks to eliminate any emotional barriers.

Then it happened—I was following Daddy without a misstep. Surprised, I exclaimed, "I can do it!"

Daddy seemed just as surprised and gave me his highest compliment, "Not bad."

I was so pleased. This happened not long before he died in 1986.

Daddy & Peggy
40ᵗʰ birthday party
Philadelphia
1983

Mom & Daddy
The Jitterbugs
Mom's pool table
in background

Quick-Start Guide: Family Genealogy & DNA Testing

I doubt there would be a story to tell, if not for a visit in 2012 to my hometown of Harrisburg, PA from St. Augustine, FL, with Noah, my nine-year-old grandson. Introducing him to relatives I had known all my life sparked my interest in genealogy.

Susan, my "half" aunt, whom I barely knew until that summer, and I began exchanging emails. She had been working on her family tree for years. She wanted me to register for a free account and accept an invitation to view her tree. Because she and my mother had the same father, the paternal side of her tree mimics one-fourth of my family tree—my maternal grandfather's line.

No matter how many times Susan reminded me that viewing her tree would be free, I wouldn't sign up because I was afraid my obsessive nature would take over and my life might be absorbed into searching for ancestors.

More than four years later, in 2016, Susan forwarded a sale notice for Ancestry.com DNA tests. I registered and bought a kit. I accepted the invitation to view her family tree and was immediately sorry I had waited so long.

This brief "how to" is for those who are eager to register for an account and submit a DNA kit.

Register for a Guest Account

1. Go to Ancestry.com
2. Click GET STARTED
3. On the next screen, click GET START-ED. You will see various options for a cost, which you can ignore.
4. On the next screen, fill in the form: First, Last Name, Email, and Password.

These details can be changed anytime via your Account settings. Remember to record the email and password.

Purchasing and activating DNA kits are two distinct activities. People often buy them as gifts for relatives and friends. Each adult is now required to sign up for an account and activate his or her own kit. The one-time cost for a DNA kit includes the laboratory analysis and access to the results. Wait for a sale, or if you're in a hurry, ask a friend with an account to invite you through Ancestry.com's referral program, which currently includes a discount for you and a gift card for your friend.

The DNA kit comes with easy-to-follow instructions for collecting spit. A unique, 16-digit code is included. Activating is the process of entering this 16-digit code into your account.

Activate a DNA Kit

These instructions are for an adult who has a registered account.

1. Upon logging in, Ancestry.com opens to a screen with a Black Bar Menu across the top: HOME, TREES, SEARCH, DNA, HELP, EXTRAS
2. Choose DNA.
3. From the drop-down menu, click on AncestryDNA.
4. On the next screen, top right corner, click on Activate a kit.
5. Click through a few screens to verify you are activating the kit for yourself until you get to a screen for entering the 15-digit code.
6. After activation, Ancestry.com sends email confirmations for each step of the process: we received your kit, your kit is at the lab, and so forth.

PART II Family Trees

Contents

10

Ashley's Family Tree

THE night I decided to open Ashley's tree plays out like a movie scene, slowly and relentlessly:

Wednesday evening, look at various combinations of shared matches.

Send messages, "How am I related to you? How are you related to Ashley?"

Hope somebody will respond.

Someone finally invites me to see a family tree.

Nothing makes sense. No one is from or has anything to do with Harrisburg.

Keep busy. Add relatives to the Martin and Nicholson sides of my tree.

Click on green leaf tree hints, view documents—marriage certificate, census record.

Early on, original handwritten records reveal complete details.

Later, only get typed indexes of records, no details.

Subscription ordering page interrupts more often—the Website wants money.

Discount offers vary between 20 to 50 percent.

Can't stand the suspense any longer.

Just before phones shut down in Utah, I reach customer service.

"Yes," she answers, "trees open immediately with a credit card payment."

Decision made to face facts.

Give the sixteen digits, loud and clear, quickly offer the expiration date.

Click on View Match beside Ashley's 144-person tree.

It's true—the receiver barely in its cradle, the tree opens immediately.

Now, nothing is between me and the names in her tree.

Heart rate and breathing return to normal.

The first thing I saw after clicking on Ashley's name was her smiling face. She was in her wedding dress standing close to her husband in his finery, both showing off their rings. I was surprised to see their names and birth dates. For privacy, the Website hides the names of living people with the word Private. The names of Ashley's sister and brother-in-law were also visible. But there were others in her tree showing as Private.

Ashley's father's name and birth date were visible, but her mother was marked Private. She has grandparents and some great-grandparents listed, but the relationship lines are confusing because many have more than one spouse. I was looking at the Family View of the tree which shows only names and dates, not birth and death locations. The Pedigree View is worse, because now I can't see siblings, only Ashley's direct family line. Opening the Profile View for each person in the tree, one by one, provided the information I needed, but the process was too time consuming. Then I found a perfect

Ashley & Josh

way to view the tree for the purpose of my search. List of All People has three-columns including (1) name, (2) birth date and place, and (3) death date and place. Scanning down the page there are mostly Illinois and Wisconsin births and deaths. Then the place, though spelled wrong, jumps out—Harrisboro D Pennsylvania. I know this means Harrisburg, my hometown. The D is for Dauphin County, where most of my relatives were born.

There he is—the only person from Pennsylvania—James Koller, born 01 May 1923, died 04 October 1988. Though not a believer that coincidences have meaning, I'm taken aback when I see he died in Florida—just over an hour from where I live now.

I returned to the Family View and found that James is Ashley's grandfather. Perhaps he is my uncle. If he is my father, the Private person representing Ashley's mother would be my half sister. A woman I don't know would be as closely related to me biologically as the two sisters I spent practically every day of my life with for eighteen years. Amazing!

Ashley's grandmother's name box was also Private. Could she still be alive? James is shown as having two other wives. There are no children listed for one. The other, almost twenty years younger than James, has a death date listed. They had two children, a son and a daughter.

I was surprised by what I found, but not for more than fifteen seconds. After my sisters and I ordered DNA kits, I began speculating, and, without meaning to, I must have prepared myself for a "surprise father." What I wasn't prepared for was a name I had never heard before. Familiar names from the crowd of friends Mom and Daddy knew were Srignoli, Poppavicki, Spahr. And Shakespeare was the one I expected to see.

I grew up knowing Mom was, at one time, in love with him. After my DNA results arrived, I even dug out my old baby book that Mom had recorded dates in for events like "rolled over," "first tooth," "said 'Mama.'" On the last page he had written *I knew you when ....* and signed it *Shakes.* Because he knew me as a baby, I had always thought the comment routine—even the unfinished sentence with dots. But the DNA match with Ashley had me ready to believe this cryptic phrase meant he "knew me" when I was conceived.

If Ashley's grandfather had been William Shakespeare (his real name), I would have understood immediately what had occurred. Though still caught off guard, this man would have meant something to me. I would have memories to share with his family. Shakes' children had probably heard about my parents and seen high school photos of them, just as I heard about and had seen—even still have—pictures of Shakes. Disappointment set in.

It was after midnight by the time I finished looking carefully through Ashley's tree to be sure James was the only person from Pennsylvania. My eyes were burning, but I couldn't go to bed without writing to Ashley. I hoped a warmer, personal message, instead of the cold ones previously sent, would elicit a response.

Date: January 25, 2017

Subject: Our relationship

Dear Ashley,

You look pretty in your wedding photos. I figured out how we are related, at least my best guess. Have any other family members contributed DNA so we can be sure?

Peggy

Susan would be excited to hear that I finally plunked down money for a subscription and that I *probably* found a *probable* answer to the mystery of Ashley. Before shutting down my computer, I whipped off an email.

Susan,

Guess what? I just joined and went into Ashley's tree. Her grandfather was born in 1923 in Harrisburg. James Koller. Mom was born in 1920. James is dead now. The names of both Ashley and her sister and even their birth dates are visible!

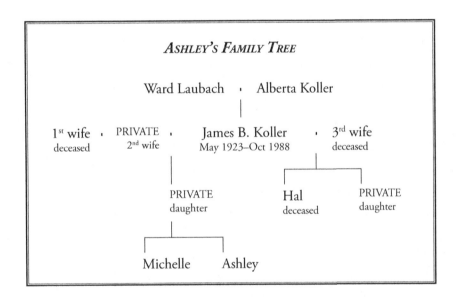

11

Sixty-Four 4th-Great-Grandparents & 100s of Cousins

THE first morning after paying for my subscription, I couldn't wait to turn on my computer and explore to my heart's desire. Instead of sitting in front of the TV as usual, reading while listening to C-Span's *Washington Journal* news and call-in program, I drank coffee in front of my Mac.

Once I could open and review tree hints, I wanted to locate more great-grandparents. I began with the names already in my tree. Emma Garman, my mother's great-grandmother, was eight years old and living with her mother and father, according to the 1870 census record. I checked the boxes with her parents' names, clicked yes to attach the record, and their names were automatically added to my tree. Tree hints appeared for each of them, which led me to their marriage and death certificates. After making sure the suggested records were about Emma's parents, I attached them. Because *their* parents' names were on the certificates, my third-great-grandparents ended up in my tree. As I continued opening, reviewing, and clicking, I soon had Emma's great-grandparents, my fourth, in my tree. If I hadn't made a mistake, I'd found my gateway ancestor, the immigrant from the Old World who established residency in the New World and began the family line that reached and passed me and has paused, for the time being, with my grandson. My sixth-great-grandfather was born J. Leonard Germann, in Germany in 1729.

I knew the term "gateway ancestor" also referred to a relative who has descended from royalty or the aristocracy. Who knows what I will find if I trace J. Leonard's background?

Along with grandparents, I added any siblings who showed up in the records. Susan doesn't understand why I do this—add these collateral relatives. She questions me, but wouldn't come right out and say, "I think you're nuts." She mostly maintains a pedigree tree—direct family lines—parents to grandparents to great-grandparents, then to great-great-grandparents, and so on. Other relatives are included if they are important to the family history. I found adding relatives engaging, and seeing the number of people increase next to my little tree symbol was gratifying.

I never thought about third-, fourth-, or fifth-great-grandparents before my DNA adventure. My maternal great-grandparents did seem real to me from listening to Mom reminisce and hearing Nana, her mother, tell me stories such as, "In the morning your mother used to go next door for Grammy Martin to cook her egg. She'd say, 'I take my gokey to Grammy's.'"

After realizing my attempt at genealogy using a spreadsheet would not make sense to my daughter, let alone my grandson, I decided to create a family tree photo book. I began with a photograph of Noah with his parents, then with his grandparents (all four were still alive), followed by him with two great-grandmothers.

I had photos back to my great-great-grandparents, at least on my mother's side. I don't

remember thinking at the time "These are Noah's fourth-great-grandparents, that makes seven generations!"

Getting all these names in my tree required hours at the computer. I came to understand why digital activity could be so appealing—it's easy, no need for paper or for sharpening pencils—each click rewarded me with more relatives or an addition to my collection of documents. Looking at the name of a sixth-great-grandparent made me feel part of an unbroken stream of life.

I wondered where this was headed, so stopped to calculate visibly: Two circles represent my parents, which leads to four grandparents, then eight greats. We—as in all of us—have 64 fourth-great-grandparents! One hundred twenty-eight fifth-great-grandparents and doubling for every generation thereafter. But the fourth are pertinent to me because it is relatively easy to find these grandparents. Record keeping by the middle of the eighteenth century was relatively good, and most are easily accessible because the documents have been digitized. All I have to do is sit at my computer and click-click.

Others might not be so lucky, but for the most part, my family lived in the same central part of Pennsylvania as their parents and grandparents. No need to track down records from all over the country, trying to trace a southern or westward migration. There are exceptions when trying to identify a DNA cousin whose ancestor, a great-great-aunt or uncle of mine, took off for parts unknown. Because my relatives were not recent immigrants, there was no need to pay for a more expensive subscription to search overseas or struggle with a foreign language, which in my case would have been German.

Then I remembered a possible new father. If this turns out to be true, I would be confronted with three sets of grandparents: (1) maternal, (2) raised-me paternal, and (3) biological paternal. Heaven only knows how many hundreds or thousands of cousins have been produced by ninety-six fourth-great-grandparents.

For the time being, I would focus on my mother's line. Learning to use the Website to develop my tree and identify DNA cousins on the maternal side of my family, the family I was most familiar with, would only help me if and when the time came to apply my skills to an unknown paternal family.

Emanuel Garber · Melinda Harriet Rice
Dec 1842–Mar 1926   Apr 1849–Aug 1908

Edward Briner · Gertrude Garber
Apr 1869–Aug 1949   Mar 1869–June 1941

Irvin Martin · Harriet Briner
Mar 1893–Dec 1948   May 1893–May 1987

Frank "Nick" Nicholson · Margaret "Marg" Martin
Oct 1920–Sep 1986   Mar 1920–Feb 2002

Victor · Peggy

John · Sherry

Noah

Marg (Mom-mom), with mom Harriet (Nana), grandmother Gertrude Briner, (front left) held by great-grandfather Emanuel Garber

Sherry, with her mom Peggy, held by grandmother Mom-mom (Marg), and great-grandmother Nana

Noah, with his mom Sherry, grandmother Peggy, held by great-grandmother Mom-mom

Tree Hints & Attaching Documents

Links to all sorts of documents—census records, birth and death certificates, service records—which may be about a person in your tree are searched for automatically and indicated by a green leaf hint on the corner of the person's name box. The total number of hints, up to 99, for all the people in your tree is shown on the right side of the Black Menu Bar.

The only way to access these specific hints is from a person's Profile View. Opening and reviewing a document gives you the opportunity to decide if the information correctly pertains to that particular person. If so, you can attach (Yes) the information (there may not be an actual document), reject it (No), or wait to decide (Maybe). Accepted records are moved to Facts. Rejected and Maybe records can be reassessed anytime by clicking on the links, Ignored and Undecided.

Most times, any additional family members listed on a document can be added to your tree automatically by check marking the little box next to the name. But if you aren't careful, you'll end up with duplicates. Make sure the person is a new person—not in your tree already with a slightly different name—by clicking on the "Not a New Person" link.

12

Ambivalent & Determined Adoptees

NEW DNA matches arrived on an irregular basis—none for days, other times three at once. Most often they were in the 4th cousin range. When the match was closer, in the 2nd or 3rd category, it was like winning a prize. M.K. showed up one day in the 3rd cousin category. Shared matches put him firmly in my grandfather Irvin Martin's line.

Off went an email to Susan to tell her before she could tell me. Susan and I were fully cooperating in solving family mysteries, but my competitive nature made it feel like a race between us. (She laughed when I mentioned this.) M.K. was the first person listed in Susan's 2nd category group.

I composed a detailed message to M.K. He didn't have a tree, but mine was filled with enough people that I was sure he could figure out how we were related. Almost always, I would add a sentence to my messages, letting a match know I would share my tree if he or she sent me an email address.

Susan also wrote to him. My messages were always direct, while Susan was more delicate and nuanced. Neither of us got a return message.

After three weeks, I received an answer from M.K. in my personal email. This was a good sign and meant to me that he was willing to be in direct contact. He apologized for taking so long to get in touch, and said he couldn't answer my question about our relationship because he had been adopted. I appreciated how open M.K. was in expressing his feelings:

I hope you understand my hesitation to learn more about my biological family. I have never pursued this mainly out of respect for the man and woman who raised me. "They are my parents" and the best people I have ever known. However, I lost my father a few years ago, and my mother now has dementia. I guess it is time for me to find out more about my biological family.

Susan received the same message and we, each in our own way, let him know we could help figure out where he belonged in our family. M.K. wrote back to say he didn't know much about his birth parents. He thought they were married when he was born and living in the same city where his father was serving in the armed forces. We were surprised to hear his adopted family had names similar to some family names we had mentioned to him. This may not be significant. Just as today, some names are popular during certain years.

But soon he stopped responding to our questions, again expressing that he didn't feel a strong need to find his birth parents. M.K.'s lack of interest made more sense when he mentioned that his daughter was the one who had bought the kit and gave it to him as a gift.

Susan is especially willing to assist those affected by adoption. She was helped recently to find a child she placed for adoption. Search Squad, one of many online organizations that help parents and children find each other, successfully reunited Susan with her daughter Beth. Literally overnight, Susan became a mother, grandmother, and great-grandmother.

The members of Search Squad who work to bring children and parents together are called "angels." An angel located Beth only days after Susan first contacted the organization. The angel posted Beth's contact information after Susan had gone to bed. All night long, members were posting comments and eagerly waiting for Susan to see the good news.

During a visit, Susan showed me these messages which were so heartfelt they would bring tears to anyone's eyes.

Search Squad, as does any reputable site, has strict policies that only the involved parties—the adopted child or parent—can contact each other. Once Susan calmed down from the excitement of knowing her daughter had been located, she emailed Beth. Susan told me what happened next: "Beth was sitting at a red light when her phone dinged. After reading the

message, she shook the whole way home. When she got there and told her husband, 'I don't know what to do.' He told her, 'Write back.' "

After many phone calls and Facebook exchanges, Beth flew to Harrisburg for her first hug with her birth mother. Luckily, they found each other in time for Susan and her longtime partner, Angie, to attend the granddaughter's wedding. Especially poignant to me is that Susan and her second great-grandchild will know each other from day one—as if the family had never been separated.

Beth had been searching for her birth mother (with support from her loving adoptive parents) for fifteen years. Not long after giving birth, Susan had returned to her home state of Pennsylvania. Beth, with no way of knowing, had used a state-wide, not a national, adoption registry. Susan and Beth wanted their story included because they hoped others

Adoption Resources

The child or parent you are searching for may test with only one company and/or register on only one adoption website. You may want to test with all major companies and register / search many websites. When exploring online, make sure you are on a reputable site. Be especially careful if money is involved. Here are a few suggestions.

DNA Testing
• Ancestry.com probably has the largest number of users and is designed to make searching/messaging user friendly. See HELP: Support Center – Finding Biological Family.
• FamilyTreeDNA.com, in addition to providing tests, accepts DNA uploads from other testing sites.
• 23 andme.com has a focus on genetic health information and uses an automatic intermediary message feature instead of direct contact between matches.
• GEDmatch.com does not do testing. This is a free site (with extra features available at a low cost) which accepts DNA uploads from other sites. The free features provide detailed comparisons of chromosome matching between and among users.

Register with Adoption Databases
• National Adoption Registry
• State sites where the birth/adoption took place, which are normally free.

Join private search groups via Facebook
• Search Squad
• DNA Detectives

in a similar situation would benefit from what they learned.

Susan wasn't the only close member of our family who "placed" a baby for adoption and later came to know and develop a relationship with the child. I used to say "gave away" or "give up" for adoption. Susan and I discussed this traditional phrasing and why it sounds so wrong. She helped me understand that, up until the last minute, a mother hopes the circumstances will mi-

Beth & Susan at Kayla's wedding June 2016

raculously change. I can't speak from experience, never having faced such a decision. Soon after I told my boyfriend I was pregnant, we eloped.

The birth records once open in Pennsylvania are now closed. Online listing services require basic information which one or the other party may not have. Beth searched in the state in which she grew up, where Susan no longer lived. Massive DNA databases overcome many of these barriers. The ease in locating a birth parent depends partially upon who in the birth family has participated in testing.

My situation was not different, but perhaps Susan, more aware of separated families, surprised me with her sensitivity.

Peggy,
I have been wondering how you are handling all of this. Finding out that you and Ronda have different fathers must be devastating.
Susan

What would have been devastating was not having Susan's involvement. We were in touch every day by email or phone, focused on the practical implications of reaching Ashley and determining my relationship to her. But more important was Susan's emotional support. I would have felt isolated and lonely without her.

February 15, 2017
Susan

I am very emotional and breaking into tears at odd moments. I can't tell you how bereft I feel. Koller wasn't one of the crowd my mom and dad hung around with. James was three years younger. If only it had been Shakes. I still can't believe it's true. The only other explanation I come up with is *there's something wrong with the DNA from either Ashley or myself. But remember, if Ronda and I were full sisters, we wouldn't be looking for a different father.*

Peggy

Yes, my situation is different. I wasn't adopted, but now I can identify a bit with that feeling—the one of wanting to know who that person was who passed on my genes. I assisted a few people to find their birth parents, and I stay in touch with others who continue to search. But people are different. Not everyone has that "feeling." Perhaps the gift of a DNA kit to her father implies that M.K.'s daughter wants to find her biological grandparents. I expect, someday when the time is right, to hear from her.

13

Long-Lived Lives Fly By

MANY DNA matches had not created trees, others had as few as five people in theirs, and some even had fifty thousand or more. I felt like a voyeur but didn't feel guilty. After all, these trees were public and the owners knew others could wander through them. Some owners made their trees private. I hated that little lock symbol which prevented me from snooping. I wanted to figure out how I was related to everyone!

Eight weeks after beginning my family tree, I had become completely addicted to being on the Website. From morning to night, I reviewed documents for people in my Martin-Nicholson family tree, looked at DNA matches, and searched through family trees trying to identify relationships. Sometimes I sent a message to someone: "Would you be willing to help find our relationship?"

I looked at people randomly and jumped from one match to another. A woman named Judith in my 4th cousin category had only twenty-two people in her tree. Smaller trees usually won't have enough generations to find a recognizable surname. This wasn't true with Judith's tree. Her great-grandmother was Elizabeth Garman from Pennsylvania. Elizabeth's father was Edward Samuel Garman, but there was no birth or death location listed for him. My third-great-grandfather was Samuel Garman. (Grandpa Martin's mother was a Garman.) Judith's Elizabeth had migrated west and my Garmans stayed in Pennsylvania, but I was confident I could figure out how we were related to each other in no time at all.

All I needed to do was find someone from Judith's Garmans who was a sibling to one of mine, and their parents would be our most recent common ancestor. But I was wrong about how much time it would take. I spent hours and still wasn't any closer to the answer. I was so frustrated with all the Edwards, Samuels, Daniels, and Johns that when a son named Adam appeared for Elizabeth

Hess and Samuel Keller Garman, I was so happy to see a unique name I decided to focus on him. This would mean going off on a tangent. I justified this by figuring the more Garmans in my tree, the better. This would make it easier and quicker to identify other DNA matches later. I could continue my search for my relationship with Judith anytime.

I relied on tree hints to get more information about Adam and his family. I examined each document to be sure it pertained to this Adam Garman. The 1870 US census showed Adam's age as eight months, the seventh child born to his parents. In 1880, Adam was ten as expected, and the family had grown to eight children with the addition of another girl. The 1890 census records were lost in a fire, but that is a story for another time.

By 1900, Adam, thirty years old, was married to Minnie, twenty-six, and they were the parents of four children. Their oldest son, William E., doesn't show up in the 1910 census. Had he died during the intervening years?

At some point before 1920, Adam and Minnie moved from East Hanover to Derry Township. They had not moved far, as both townships were in Dauphin County. Their youngest daughter was still at home at twenty-one years old, and another daughter, who first showed up as a four-year-old in 1900, has returned home with her husband and two children.

In 1930, the daughter with the children is still at home, but the husband evidently is not living with them anymore. What happened to him? Abandonment, divorce, death?

The latest census available online is 1940. Adam, at seventy-one, was still listed as "head," along with his wife who is sixty-six years old. Often I have found many elderly parents, by that age—especially if they are widowed—living with one of their children. Husbands are always listed as head of family, women only if no man is present. The relationships refer to the head of house, so if an elderly father is living with his married daughter, he would be listed as father-in-law.

Adam Hess Garman, according to a Social Security Death Index, began life on November 12, 1869 and died September 22, 1952. According to the death certificate, he died from arteriosclerotic cardiovascular renal disease which had begun ten years earlier. Other significant conditions listed were "amputation right leg above knee for Buerger's disease with gangrene." Though this document was the only place Adam's middle name was listed, it conforms with the tradition of using the mother's maiden name as a middle name for one or more of the children.

Adam's death certificate was useful for tying up a loose end. The "informant" on a death certificate is usually a close relative of the deceased. Though the relationship is not specified, sometimes just the name can clear up a mystery. The informant in this case was Adam's

What is that Little Green Leaf?

Tree Hints & Shared Ancestor Hints

A little green leaf is the symbol for both Tree Hints and Shared Ancestor Hints.

A Tree Hint indicates there is a document, story, or photo waiting for review about a person in your tree. This leaf appears on the corner of the person's name box but can only be accessed from the Profile View. Tree hints have nothing to do with DNA.

A Shared Ancestor Hint indicates you and a DNA Match have a common ancestor in your respective trees. The leaf appears across from the display name of your DNA Match next to View Match. Whether this is a correct relationship or not is dependent on the accuracy of the trees.

If you have a tree, Tree Hints will appear. If you have a common ancestor, Shared Ancestor Hints will appear. But a Subscription is required to open and view the hints.

son W. Eugene Garman. William E. was last seen as a six-year-old on the 1900 census. William had not died, as I speculated, but lived to adulthood as Eugene. He would have been sixteen in 1910. It was not unusual for teenage children to live with other families, boys working as laborers or farmers' helpers and girls as servants.

I'm not sure how to describe my feelings as I sit back and look at the long list of documents linked to Adam in my tree. I traveled with him from the beginning of his life, saw him married, watched his children grow up and move out of the house, and visualized him working as a carpenter. At the end, I had to say goodbye. He was here and gone in not much more than half an hour.

Life and living felt concrete as I viewed the records that proved Adam and his family existed.

Here was proof that before he died, his children had produced the next generation. But I couldn't avoid the sense of mortality I felt for Adam and myself—for any of us—for the brief time we have been given on this earth. A life that required only minutes to document.

Now Adam's family was firmly inserted in my tree, but I wasn't any closer to finding the connection between Judith and me. But the urge was strong to keep going, a few taps on the keyboard to enter key data points and I would have ten to twelve hints for Adam's son Eugene. Depending upon the way he lived, one marriage or more, living in one county or moving around, I could proceed to scan Eugene's entire life from birth to death, instead of getting to bed at a decent hour.

14

Census Records & Their Stories

I was working my way through the documents which recorded the existence of Samuel H. Garman from my maternal grandfather's side of the family. Besides loving the process of adding relatives to my tree, I was trying to determine how two DNA matches, Karen and her brother, R.L., siblings to each other, were related to me. In my tree, I connected them to me, but only through marriage. The tree diagram showed them as "first cousins four times removed of wife of first cousin six times removed." Based on the amount of DNA we share, I expect we are third cousins.

The 1870 census was the first available, listing Samuel as fourteen years old, living with his mom and dad and six siblings in Lebanon County, PA. In 1880, Samuel, at twenty-four, was boarding with a family near Hershey and working as a laborer.

Samuel must have fallen in love because by 1900 he was married to Lizzie. There were four children—18-year-old Harry, 8-year-old twin boys,

and a daughter, Annie, 9. I wondered about the nine-year gap between Harry and Annie. Children often arrived every few years or so. It wasn't unusual to see consecutive years listed on census records.

Accessing the 1910 census, I was right to question the interval after Harry and before Annie, who was now 20. Perhaps the three additional daughters, ages 24, 23, and 21, had been sent out to work. Girls as young as twelve years old could be found living with other families and referred to as "servant" on the census record. Still living at home were Harry and the twins.

When I first began researching and encountered so many yearly births, I was amazed. The appearance of yearly births was partly a function of how ages were determined by the census rules—age at last birthday before the day of the census. Looking at the actual dates revealed that many times there were approximately two years between births. I'm not implying anything is wrong with having children two years apart, but to the modern eye it was overwhelming to see how many women had ten to fourteen or more children in so few years.

By 1920, all but one daughter had left home. A boy with a different surname listed as a son in 1910 was, as I had surmised, a grandson. But the daughter's last name remained Garman. Who knows what the story is and what difficulties this situation creates for genealogists and DNA descendants.

When I opened the 1930 record there was one long list of names, in alphabetical order. Samuel was seventy-three years old and the address on the top of the form was Pennsylvania State Lunatic Hospital. In previous decades, he had been noted as son, laborer, and head. Here he was listed as inmate.

~ *MEMORY* ~

I know that place by another name—the Harrisburg State Hospital. The official name changed a few times, but we who grew up in the 1940–'50s knew the place was for lunatics, no matter how much they cleaned up the name. As an adult, I learned that people with all kinds of diagnoses other than mental illnesses were confined, including developmentally delayed, back then known as mentally retarded.

The hospital closed in 2006, but the hundred eighty-three acres and many of the buildings are still there. Most of the farmland where the involuntary residents used to grow their own food is leased by the State to private growers. The brick buildings are used for government offices.

When in Harrisburg, sometimes I drove through the grounds on my way from seeing one relative to visiting another. Once I tried to identify the building I worked in as a teacher's aide in 1971. Twenty-eight years old, newly divorced, with two children, I was a full-time student at Harrisburg Area Community College and working part time in the hospital's Education Unit.

When I saw those words—Pennsylvania State Lunatic Hospital—on

the census record, it reminded me of my mother's threats. We drove past the hospital on the way to visit my grandmother who lived in the city. Mom didn't say it every week, but often enough: "We'll put you *there*" or "You'll end up *there*, locked in like Uncle Hen." This scared me because I had known him as a nice man who showed cartoons from a movie projector on the living room wall during parties or when I stayed overnight with Anne Marie.

When Mom mentioned Uncle Hen and me in the same sentence, I was terrified. I didn't know him as a strange, crazy person who needed to be locked away. Here was proof that normal people could end up going crazy. My temperament—screaming and arguing—was the reason for her threats.

Even as a young adult, I remembered that fear—the fear I *could* end up in a padded cell. Perhaps this was what led me to choose to study psychology at HACC. Some five years later, while earning a master's degree, an internship dedicated to family systems theory helped me understand that my "temper tantrums" were most likely the result of my mother's unreliable and inconsistent behavior.

The only problem is she's dead and gone, and I'm left with an unwanted pattern of behavior—too loud and insistent when someone lies or uses irrational reasoning. A pattern that only worked with my mother.

~ ~ ~ ~

Recently, I called Anne Marie to find out what Uncle Hen's diagnosis was. Turns out her father wasn't mentally ill. He had had a stroke. He was locked up for throwing a table at her two younger brothers. The stroke left him placid and childlike, unable to work. Until the incident, they cared for him at home for a few years. The police gave Aunt

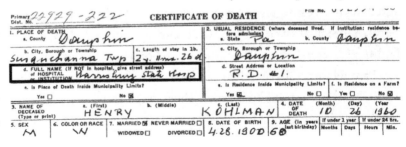

Notes About US Census Records

Ancestry.com has blank census forms available from 1790 to 1940 to view online or download. Having these forms in front of me with easy to read headings (questions asked) helped me understand the hand-written completed records much faster. My curiosity about why the census forms varied every ten years led me to the US Census Bureau website where I found fascinating explanations.

My experience was mostly with how the census records were completed in central Pennsylvania. For some jurisdictions every column was completed, while for others many items were left blank. Households by address (not necessarily by family) were enumerated. The head of the family, along with a surname, was listed first. Husbands were "heads" unless a wife had been widowed. Other family members followed with children in descending order by age. Servants and boarders, if there were any, came last. A different surname was added as necessary for a married daughter or non-family members. When relationships were noted, they were in reference to the head of household. For example, if the wife's mother was living with the couple, the relationship was listed as "mother-in-law."

I was taken back in time reading the words used in some questions: "Deaf, dumb, blind, or insane?" and "Whether maimed, crippled, bedridden, or otherwise disabled." With no idea of the purposes for collecting this information, I noticed the assumption that answering "Yes" for either question didn't distinguish among the terms. It's as if the ability of a person to function independently was irrelevant. Or that services for special needs could be lumped together. Was it assumed that education or healthcare for people who are blind or insane would be the same? I wondered what they meant by crippled: walking with a cane?

Questions varied from one ten-year period to the next. By 1920 a question about service in the Union or Confederate army or navy had been dropped. I was sorry when the question about the number of children born and the number still living to a woman was eliminated. Another asked how long a couple had been married. At one time, there were questions about the year of naturalization and mother tongue.

Collecting names for family trees is not always straight forward. First and middle names are sometimes reversed from one census record to another. You may never know what name was on the birth certificate (if there was one), Walter Oliver or Oliver Walter—both versions can be found among census, death, and marriage records. But be careful. It is not unheard of for a family to use such a format for two different children—make sure children in the same family were born and died on different dates. Keep an eye out for a change in a name—you may find Walter O. in the 1900 census at six years old and think he disappeared or died, until you realize W. Oliver at sixteen is the "missing" child.

Changes in international boundaries following World War I, caused confusion for those from Austria-Hungary, Germany, Russia, or Turkey. Only the name of the country was to be entered instead of naming a province, state, or region.

Annie (Daddy's sister) a choice between the hospital or jail.

Anne Marie and her mother visited every week, until Uncle Hen died, two years after being committed. According to Samuel Garman's tombstone he died in 1934, his wife in 1922. Perhaps Samuel had a stroke or was senile and she cared for him at home till then. If so, he would have been locked up for twelve long years.

I learned a bit about Samuel and the sad ending to his life, but I haven't yet found a common ancestor to correctly represent my DNA relationship to Karen and her brother, R.L. I expect to find one sooner or later.

15

History Comes Alive

USING tree hints wasn't the only way to find ancestors. Once I identified how I was related to someone, even a fifth cousin, I put our common ancestor in my tree, unless he or she was already there, and then filled in the descendants until I got to the identified cousin. Quite often, this cousin or one of the relatives in between had found great-grandparents or documents, which I had not yet come across.

I had worked backwards from my mother, Marg, to her great-grandmother, Melinda Harriet, and eventually reached my sixth-great-grandparents Abigail and Zachariah Rice.

Both Abigail and Zachariah were born in Germany, where the name was spelled Reis. This was progress toward my goal of identifying from which country my four grandparents' ancestors emigrated. This took care of my maternal grandmother on her mother's side. Given Nana's father was a Briner, that side was almost certainly from Germany too.

There are many delightful stories, true or not, posted by family members in the Gallery part of family trees (see Profile View). These are often shown as tree hints. I've included a long piece I found about Abigail's and Zachariah's involvement in the Revolutionary War. Though there may be family myth woven into the story, reading about my own family involved in historical events was exciting. (See "Abigail Hartman Rice, Revolutionary War Nurse," *Journal of the American Revolution*, November 28, 2016, for a documented story.)

Zachariah Rice (Reis), born in Bavaria, Germany in 1731, decided to seek a better life in the "New World." At the age of twenty, already a skilled carpenter and millwright, he boarded the British ship Edinburgh, which docked in Philadelphia on September 16, 1751. Zachariah settled in southeast Pennsylvania where he designed and constructed a mill to separate clover seed, the first of its kind in the New World. It was the prototype for many others that would be built during the next eighty years.

In 1757, Zachariah married Marie Appolonia "Abigail" Hartman. Abigail was born in Württemberg, Germany. During their marriage of thirty-three years, Abigail gave birth to twenty-one children, seventeen of whom survived to adulthood.

Zachariah Rice enlisted in the Continental Army as an engineer and carpenter under the command of General George Washington. He helped build the Yellow Springs Hospital in Chester County, which would soon be used as a field hospital for the casualties of the war.

In September 1777, during his retreat from the Battle of Brandywine, Washington and his officers stopped at the Rice farm and asked Abigail if they could have some water. She sent one of her daughters to retrieve a pitcher of water from their well, to which she added some sugar, spices, and rum, making a drink that was popularly known as "flip." When Abigail handed the drink to Washington, "Here, my Lord," he replied, "We have no titles here, we are all brothers."

As General Washington drank this beverage, Abigail's five-year-old daughter, Susannah, approached him. Washington smiled, picked her up and sat her on his knee while he finished his drink.

After filling in the ancestors from the Rices to me, I had to admit that arithmetic didn't give me the correct number of fourth-great-grandparents. First cousins Sarah and Samuel married each other. This means Abigail and Zachariah are my grandparents "twice." I was naïve not to realize earlier that such cousin marriages took place—and still do.

Many of the Rice descendants joined the Sons of the American Revolution or the Daughters of the American Revolution. The completed applications are bursting with names, birth and death dates, and marriage details. Gathering the materials and applying for membership for myself and my daughter in the DAR and for my grandson in the SAR would be a fun project.

I wonder if I'm the only one fascinated by this form of recreation brought about by scientific and technological changes that allow non-scientists access to DNA data. I didn't think up the term "recreation," it was on the internet in an article about the popularity and use of DNA testing. And I speculate if the search for my relationship to these fourth and fifth cousins, which I admit is a meaningless activity, is a way to avoid thinking about Ashley's unresponsiveness and the possibility that I may not make any progress in *that* search.

Calculating Complexity

Endogamy

When people had large families and lived in the same geographic location, marriages between blood relations were bound to happen. As in the Rice case, the marriage was between two people within one family. There are also cases of more than one person from a family marrying into another family. I heard of a family in which three sisters married three brothers. These situations increase the amount of shared DNA in descendants above the expected average. In other words, two people will seem more closely related than they actually are.

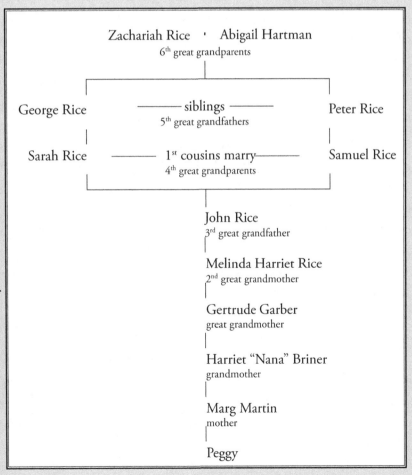

Zachariah Rice · Abigail Hartman
6th great grandparents

———— siblings ————
5th great grandfathers

George Rice   Peter Rice

Sarah Rice ———— 1st cousins marry ———— Samuel Rice
4th great grandparents

John Rice
3rd great grandfather

Melinda Harriet Rice
2nd great grandmother

Gertrude Garber
great grandmother

Harriet "Nana" Briner
grandmother

Marg Martin
mother

Peggy

16

Facts Fit the Father

Four days had passed since paying for a subscription to see Ashley's tree. My time had been absorbed by peering into the trees of my DNA matches and adding to the growing number of ancestors on my mother's lineage. I loved seeing new names appear: Nana's paternal grandmother was a Kiner before she married. This was exactly what I thought I would be doing. I didn't expect to be searching for mystery genetic relatives.

After sending Ashley a more personal message, I was sure I would hear back. No such luck. I decided to go ahead and research James and his family. DNA can only be linked to one tree, so I debated with myself about putting him in mine or beginning another tree. Without more evidence, it was too disturbing to plunk him next to my mother. Within a few minutes of creating the new tree using James' birth and death dates from Ashley's tree, I had hints. The first was a census record which listed James as adopted. As if I weren't distressed enough. Daddy is probably not my biological father, this potential father has an unfamiliar name, and now I might be faced with never knowing who my paternal grandparents were.

That's silly. I do know who my "real" grandparents were—the ones I grew up with—Grandma and Grandpa Nicholson. Without that, placing babies in the loving care of others and choosing this form of parenting wouldn't happen. Adoption wouldn't make sense if strands of matching DNA were a prerequisite for love. But I wonder why a DNA connection does feel important. There were several adoptions in our family, the placing of, not the taking in kind. Years later, I experienced the joy, along with the

mothers who were reunited with their adult children. These apparent strangers instantly feel like family because of those genetic strands.

In the 1930 census, Elwood and Alberta Koller were listed with two sons: James, six years, adopted son, and Robert, not yet three. Without more information, I can't be sure if James is the adopted child of both parents or only of Elwood.

By the 1940 US census, there was a third son, Donald, and all three boys were labeled "son." If James is the biological child of Alberta, the two younger boys would be his half brothers. There are a lot of "ifs," but *if* James is my biological father, the children and grandchildren of Robert and Donald, *if* there are any, would show up in my DNA matches, *if* they were tested.

Ashley had three wives listed for James, and I found records for three marriages. City directories showed James' residence in Harrisburg for a few years. Other records indicated he lived for much of his life in Illinois. There were documents confirming he was living in Florida when he died.

Susan was looking at the same information and had a hypothesis about the adoption.

Date: January 26, 2017

Peggy,

I think I figured out the adoption thing. On Ashley's tree, she lists James' mother as Alberta Karschner and father as Ward Laubach. On the 1930 census, his parents are listed as Alberta and Elwood Koller. I think Alberta is the same person, and Ward having died, Alberta married Elwood, who then adopted James.

Susan

KOLLER FAMILY 1930 & 1940 CENSUS RECORDS

Frank H.	*Daughter*				✓	F	W	12	S		*Pennsylvania*	*Pennsylvania*
Elwood E.	Head	R	19	no	M	W	23	M	21	no	Yes	Pennsylvania	Pennsylvania
Alberta M	Wife-H			✓	F	W	24	M	16	no	Yes	Pennsylvania	Pennsylvania
James B.	adopted Son			✓	M	W	6	S		Yes	Pennsylvania	Pennsylvania
Robert E.	Son			✓	M	W	2 4/5		no	Pennsylvania	Pennsylvania

KOLLER. ELWOOD E.	Head	M	W	33	M	No.	N-1	Penna
ALBERTA M.	Wife	F	W	34	M	No.	1	Penna
JAMES B.	Son.	M	W	16	S	Yes	1	Penna
ROBERT E.	Son	M	W	12	S	Yes	7	Penna
DONALD L.	Son.	M	W	6	S	No.	0	Penna

Susan's email made sense. Scrolling through family trees of the DNA matches I shared with Ashley, the repetition of surnames and birth places was noticeable. But I didn't see any Laubachs. As yet I had no way to make sense of the information.

I had opened, reviewed, and added most of the census and other records for James. I clicked on the next-to-last hint—Application for World War II Compensation. The handwritten form was filled out in black pen with red marks correcting the dates James served stateside and overseas. He joined the service on December 7, 1942, and his address was 1716 N. Fifth Street. Marg, a bride of nine months, whose young husband was in the service, was staying with her mother practically around the corner from his home. Here was proof James was in Harrisburg at the time I was conceived.

Now what? What if Ashley never responds? There is my DNA relationship with her and documentation that James lived near my mother. Are these few facts enough to confirm James Koller was my biological father? And because he seems to be, how will I learn about him and his family—uncles, sisters, nieces—people I'm biologically linked with?

PART III Kinship

Contents

17

Tangled Branches in Family Trees

In addition to finding the family James grew up with, if the census record listing him as adopted was accurate, finding his biological father would be important to me. The Ward Laubach that Ashley had as James' father in her tree would be my biological grandfather. Where had he lived? Did he remarry and have children? If so, I might have more aunts, uncles, and cousins. Susan, the master researcher, was already hot on the trail.

Date: January 26, 2017

Subject: your grandfather?

Peggy

I found a Ward Laubach born in Northampton as was an Asher W. Laubach. You have several matches with people who have Laubach in their trees.

My great-great-grandmother Sarah Solome Ebert who married George Kiner was also from Northampton. Not that that means anything, but sometimes these connections show that families did know each other. Have you had any luck getting in touch with Ashley?

Susan

Susan would agree that, like me, she was addicted to identifying relatives and tracing long-gone ancestors. She's had years for her genealogical research to settle into a routine, and she might have had her impulses under control until seduced by my mystery. I was glad she began the search for my potential grandfather even before we knew whether or not James was my father. The challenge with genealogical research is staying focused on one person or family at a time. Though at times, looking for someone can lead to another with amazing results.

Date: January 27, 2017

Hi Peggy

Yes, it is 1 a.m. and I should be getting ready for bed but I just discovered the wildest thing (not about your possible father). I AM RELATED TO HARRIET!

When I first started working on the Martins and saw that Harriet's last name was Briner, I started looking at Briner trees (because my mother's roommate from college was a Briner).

Fast-forward to tonight. While searching for James' father, I sidetracked to the Briner trees to look at other surnames and was shocked to come across my third-great-grandparents who are on my mother's side, Sarah Salome and George Kiner.

Their daughter, Mary Ann, married a Briner. The child from that marriage, Edward Briner, was Harriet's father, thus making me related to Harriet.

Isn't that crazy!

Susan

This means Susan and I are related to each other on both sides of her family—paternal and maternal and both sides of my maternal grandparents.

Tangled Branches & Kinship Diagram

A feature referred to in the HELP: Support Center as "viewing relationship to me" shows your relationship to each person in your family tree. To see the intervening relatives, click on the link immediately below a person's name on his or her Profile View. The "Kinship Diagram" (the phrase I use for this feature is not found in the Support Center) shows only one relationship at a time with the closest taking priority.

Susan, as my tree was currently constructed, is shown as my aunt with the intervening relatives listed from Susan to her father Irvin, to his daughter Marg, ending with me. (I wonder if Ancestry.com will ever use the term "half" when appropriate?)

While searching for my biological grandfather, Susan discovered she was also related through her mother's side of the family to my grandmother

---

SUSAN AS PEGGY'S AUNT

Susan Martin
aunt
∨
Irvin Young Martin (1893–1948)
Father of Susan Martin
∨
Margaret 'Marg' Briner Martin/Nicholson (1920–2003)
Daughter of Irvin Young Martin
∨
Margaret 'Peggy' Nicholson
You are the daughter of Margaret Briner Martin/Nicholson

Harriet—her father's ex-wife! I wanted this relationship in my tree so I added Susan's mother Alice, along with her mother and her grandmother. Susan's great-grandmother, Elizabeth Kiner Lightner, my third-great-aunt, was already in my tree. Elizabeth was sister to my great-great-grandmother Mary Ann Kiner Briner. Their parents, Sarah Salome and George Kiner, were Susan's and my third-great-grandparents.

To accomplish my goal of seeing fourth cousin listed under Susan's name and view the relationship with the kindship diagram, I used EDIT: Edit Relationships. (This feature is mostly used for correcting relationship mistakes in a tree.)

Edit Relationships Example:

- On Susan's Profile View, I went to EDIT: Edit Relationships (top, right).
- To temporarily disable the "aunt" relationship, I unlinked Irvin as Susan's father.
- Clicking the X eliminated the relationship but did NOT delete the person.
- To get the software to recognize the change, I "refreshed" the screen.
- Susan's kinship to me had changed from aunt to fourth cousin.
- After copying the fourth cousin diagram to show here, I re-connected Susan's father using EDIT: Edit Relationships in reverse. I selected Add Father, then Select Someone in Your Tree. (Be sure to use the exact spelling of the person you are reconnecting. Do not add a new person.)
- After refreshing the screen, the kinship label had returned to aunt.

SUSAN & PEGGY AS FOURTH COUSINS

Susan Martin
4th cousin
∨
Alice Lee Tate/Martin/Garman (1908–1996)
Mother of Susan Martin
∨
Florence Ethel Sundy/Tate (1881–1968)
Mother of Alice Lee Tate/Martin/Garman
∨
Anna B Lightner/Sundy (1854–1937)
Mother of Florence Ethel Sundy/Tate
∨
Elizabeth Jane Kiner/Lightner (1827–1876)
Mother of Anna B Lightner/Sundy
∨
George Kiner Sr (1795 –1853)
Father of Elizabeth Jane Kiner/Lightner
∨
Mary Anna 'Annie' Kiner/Briner (1826–1910)
Daughter of George Kinger Sr
∨
Edward George Briner (1869–1949)
Son of Mary Anna 'Annie' Kiner/Briner
∨
Harriet May 'Nana' Briner/Martin/Cless (1893–1987)
Daughter of Edward George Briner
∨
Margaret 'Marg' Briner Martin/Nicholson (1920–2003)
Daughter of Harriet May 'Nana' Briner/Martin/Cless
∨
Margaret 'Peggy' Nicholson
You are the daughter of Margaret Briner Martin/Nicholson

We share an aunt-niece relationship through her father, my maternal grandfather, Irvin. We are fourth cousins, sharing third-great-grandparents through Alice, her mother. Susan and I are unsure if Harriet and Alice knew they were second cousins once removed.

I knew they were friends before the divorce. The two couples—Harriet and Irvin and Alice and her first husband—played cards and went out dancing together. My grandmother told me she divorced my grandfather because "he was runnin' with Alice." After the divorce, Irvin married Alice, and a few years later they had Susan.

In all the stories my grandmother told me, she never mentioned being related to Alice. Susan said her mom didn't mention it either. This isn't really surprising since many of us don't know who our second cousins are, let alone those once or twice removed.

Perhaps there is an official name for this phenomenon of being related to someone from both sides of your family—I'm thinking of it as a "double" relationship. In our situation, the discovery led to laughs, but has little significance. Before we participated in DNA testing or created extended family trees, Susan and I knew how we were related.

What if we had been strangers, either because of adoption or unknown fathers? Susan and I shared such a high amount of DNA that if we had found the fourth cousin relationship first, we would have kept looking. In cases involving smaller amounts, significant relationships could be overlooked.

For people trying to unravel mysteries or dealing with adoption, being aware of this phenomenon could be important. Finding one may stop the search for another, more meaningful, relationship.

18

The Martins: Like Father, Like Daughter?

ONE day a Debra Martin appeared as a 3rd cousin to me and a 2nd cousin to Susan. When neither heard back from the messages we separately sent, Susan and I asked each other, "Why doesn't Debra answer?" Our individual messages had pointed out how close our match was and expressed interest in finding out how we were related. Knowing she had just received her DNA results, I couldn't understand why she wasn't as eager as we were to communicate.

I was impatient to identify how Debra was related to the Martins. She could be "proof" that a story about Irvin, my grandfather, was true. Many, many years ago, for a college history course, the assignment was to "interview the oldest woman you know." I chose Nana, my eighty-three-year-old grandmother, who told me the story of her life. I

transcribed the audiotape and submitted it, with limited editing, as a dialog between the two of us. Whenever she referred to my grandfather, her ex-husband, Nana never called him by name. Irvin was always "he" or "your grandfather."

Harriet and Irvin married in 1914, which places the incident she talks about around 1917.

Nana: He [Irvin] started to run around when we were on Ellerslie Street. We were married only three years when he had a baby to some girl. At the bakery out there on 13th Street where that fountain is, he laid her back of the counter. Well, we were only married three years. That was when we were in the candy business.

Peggy: And you found out about it?

Nana: Yes, the lawyer called me up about it. They wanted $1000. "Where was I going to get

$1000," I said. I told him I couldn't afford to pay that. Your Grandpa was in jail.

Peggy: You mean they arrested him without telling you, then called you up and demanded the money before they would let him out!?!

Nana: Yes. I tell you that was something to go through. I didn't want his people [Irvin's parents] to know. They were so nice. They had all this family and everything [sic].

Well, we were only married three years. Your mother wasn't born yet. Anyway, when this lawyer called up, I had to do something. I told Harv [Irvin's brother] and his wife but I said, "Don't say a word to anybody. I wouldn't want Mom and Pop [her in-laws, parents of Harv and Irvin] to know anything about it."

We went up to Aunt Maggie's and I told her that Harv wanted to buy new furniture. I asked if she could loan him $600 on a note and put it in your grandpa's and my name. He would pay us and we would pay her. I got the lawyer down to $600, that's all the lower he would go. Aunt Maggie always had plenty of money upstairs in her trunk.

It was a girl baby she had. Then later on in years she moved over to Carlisle I heard.

Given how we know the police treated women when their reports involved sex, the story seems strange to me. Why would the police take the word of a woman that this particular man got her pregnant, especially a respectable, married man? But I have nothing more to go on than what Nana told me.

If there were a child, she would be about 100-years old if still alive. Age aside, we knew Susan and Debra were not half sisters because they didn't share enough DNA. Could Debra be a half niece or half great niece to Susan?

Without hearing from Debra, we grew more curious. Six weeks had passed since the first messages, and I hoped my additional messages hadn't irritated her. Late one evening, I decided there was nothing to lose by being explicit, so in my next message I brought up the possibility of an out-of-wedlock birth.

Dear Debra,

Hoping you will see one of these messages. I am writing you again because I have added people to my Martin family tree and hope we can identify how we are related. You are one of my closest DNA matches. You are even closer to my half aunt Susan Martin (who wrote to you previously).

Because of all the family matches with you, we know you are in my grandfather's line. Curious if you are a descendant of a baby he had that wasn't with my grandma—though we don't know if that really happened.

If you are getting my messages but prefer not to, please let me know.

Peggy

In Holland, where I lived for six years, I was happy to learn there was no such thing as an illegitimate baby. The US birth certificates I was coming across had a box to check, legitimate or not.

My provocation worked to finally get a one-sentence response from Debra.

Hi

Who is your grandfather?

Thinking I was on the right track that she was Irvin's descendant, I replied immediately.

Debra,

My grandfather is Irvin Martin, but he would not have had the baby with either of the wives in my tree.

Members of our family have welcomed back into our lives children who were placed for adoption. For me, DNA results have been a shock, and I would be glad to share more with you when we are in contact. Susan and I would be so happy to know another relative who is close to us.

Peggy

At first I was confused by her next question. Debra must not have gotten the gist of my message. This wasn't the first time I ran into that problem. From then on, I decided to keep my messages as short and to the point as possible.

Peggy,

Did your grandfather say her name was Viola McBride? I was trying to figure out your age to determine where we fit on a time line.

Debra

I replied that I had no way of knowing if my grandfather did father a child out of wedlock, let alone know the woman's name. To help with the time line, I listed the generations, which sometimes were as important as ages in determining relationships.

Debra,

Gen 1: Harriet is my grandma who told me the story about my grandpa, Irvin Martin, but never said the name of the woman he had the baby with.

Gen 2: Harriet and Irvin had Marg and Doris in the early 1920s.

After my grandparents divorced, Irvin married Alice and had Susan in 1948.

Gen 3: From 1943 to 1948, Marg had my sisters and me, and Aunt Doris had three boys.

Gen 4: Our (the girls, the boys, and Susan) children were born from 1962 on.

If the dates work, Irvin would be your great-grandpa.

Does that make sense, given which relatives are known and which are the mystery? Have you checked to see how much DNA you share with your top Martin matches? You are welcome to call me if that would be easier.

Peggy

All this time, I was adding spouses and children to Irvin's siblings. Susan's years of experience were a great help. She made a chart showing which cousins Debra shared DNA with, and when available, included the amount of cMs, The chart indicated that Debra was at least a descendant of Elizabeth Brenner and Simon Martin, Irwin's grandparents. I offered to send Debra an invitation to see my tree and was pleased she accepted. Her next message showed her willingness to share information.

Peggy

I started a Martin tree this morning for my dad. I was able to use the records my mother gathered.

Debra

I felt sure we were getting close to solving the mystery of Irvin's supposed indiscretion. I wrote to Debra to get clarification:

Debra,

I read over your emails to see if I understand what is known and not known – am I clear that it is your father who doesn't know who his father was?

Peggy

Her answer was short and sweet and ended the need for further detective work. No illegitimacy was involved, nor was there a mystery to begin with—just slow and garbled communication.

Peggy

My dad knows his father was Clinton, and my great-grandfather was Samuel. That would make you and my father cousins.

Debra

Nana & Aunt Maggie

Be Patient: Digitizing & Indexing

Ancestry.com is a massive site and the company is constantly adding databases and documents. Sometimes when I call the help line, a technical advisor admits that there are problems the company doesn't yet know how to solve. Not all features operate in real-time—the Website doesn't update immediately. You will become aware of this process of "indexing" when one or more of your DNA Circles disappear only to reappear a week later. I've come across a Shared Ancestry Hint attached to a match, but no common ancestor was revealed.

Documents are constantly being digitized. I've had people in my tree for over a year with few hints, when all of a sudden, ten arrive overnight. One day, there was a new hint for my grandmother—a death certificate labeled as a still birth on October 3rd. Nana told me more than once, "I had six miscarriages before your mother was born and then another one before Doris was born." I had no idea she was far enough along in any of those seven pregnancies to require a death certificate. It touched my heart to see the words—Baby Martin and still birth.

Later in the week, looking at the transcript of the oral history I had of Nana telling me the story of her life, I came across her description of the event, "…the baby was born dead on October 3rd. Grammy [her mother-in-law] said, 'Oh, it's all mortified, it's all black.' It had coal black hair, its eyes were closed, I don't know what color they were. It had no fingernails or toenails. It had a pretty little round face. It was a girl."

The year on the death certificate was 1915, she was twenty-two years old when it happened. My notes were from the recording made in 1973 of Nana telling me the story of her life. She was eighty years old then. With the passing of years, the sharpness of the pain from losing a child—known for many years or only a few months squirming inside—may diminish, but the memory attaches for a lifetime.

Yes, Debra was correct, her father and I are third cousins. Her great-grandfather Samuel and my grandfather Irvin were first cousins. Their parents were brothers, George and Joseph, respectively. Our most recent common ancestors were their parents—her third-great and my great-great-grandparents Elizabeth and Simon Martin.

Debra called to let me know her delay in responding to messages was because she has limited time for genealogy. She was busy with work and keeping an eye on her father who, at eighty-two years old, was living with her. Her great-grandfather Samuel moved west from Harrisburg around 1900. He stopped in Indiana but ended up in Chicago, working for the Miller Brewing Company. Before hanging up, Debra reminded me to let her know if I ever get proof that Nana's story is true.

I rummaged among my papers and read over my grandmother's complaints about my grandfather's philandering, which included a few more stories I hadn't remembered. In the same section, she had launched into a story about Irvin's sister Pearl. "She was running with the sheriff. She had a nice husband, he was swell, but she was the same as your grandpa. All the Martins prettin'er run around."

It wouldn't have occurred to me, but my friend Jae reminded me, "Your mother was also a Martin." I wasn't really ready to imagine my mother as having had an extra-marital encounter.

Boyd, holding Jackie, Pearl Harriet & Irvin with Marg Atlantic City ~1925

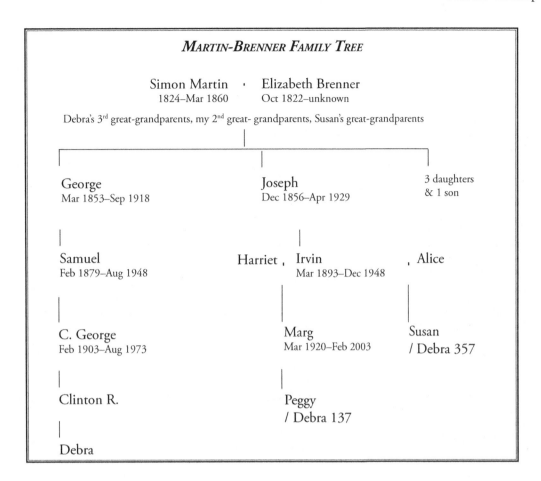

MARTIN-BRENNER FAMILY TREE

Simon Martin · Elizabeth Brenner
1824–Mar 1860   Oct 1822–unknown

Debra's 3rd great-grandparents, my 2nd great-grandparents, Susan's great-grandparents

George   Joseph   3 daughters
Mar 1853–Sep 1918   Dec 1856–Apr 1929   & 1 son

Samuel   Harriet · Irvin   · Alice
Feb 1879–Aug 1948   Mar 1893–Dec 1948

C. George   Marg   Susan
Feb 1903–Aug 1973   Mar 1920–Feb 2003   / Debra 357

Clinton R.   Peggy
                      / Debra 137

Debra

19

Hooray for Social Media!

THE intrigue about the Martins served as a good distraction for a while. But as soon as the search was over, my disappointment that I hadn't heard back from Ashley hit me like a collapsed genealogy tree. About to give up hope, super sleuth Susan came to the rescue.

Date: January 28, 2017

Peggy,

I found Ashley's Facebook page. I know it's the right one because the sister's name is the same as the one in Ashley's tree. Her fb is very public—her mother's name is Cindy.

Susan

Susan's comment about Ashley's openness on social media lead me to believe it wasn't an accident that certain names in Ashley's tree on Ancestry.com were visible. She must have discovered that checking "deceased" allowed the names, not the word "Private," to be viewed by the public, Whether I was right or wrong, I was so relieved that Susan found another way for me to reach out to Ashley.

I have a Facebook account, but almost never sign in. Emails alerting me that photos had been posted used to lure me to the site, and a minute later I would look at the clock and notice an hour had disappeared. Finally, I found a way to block those unwanted interruptions. Facebook can be useful. I wanted to apologize to a high school classmate who had an unusual first name. Google search found her immediately, but I had to join Facebook to send a message.

From that one purpose years ago, I ended up with ninety-nine friends! Many are from my high school graduating class, the rest, close friends and family. I don't confirm acquaintances. Though now it seems I ought to make it an even hundred. On the other hand, with the repeated breaches of privacy, maybe I'll "unfriend" Facebook altogether.

After reading Susan's email, I immediately logged into Facebook and located Ashley's account. To find out if James Koller is my biological father, Ashley's mother and I must compare our DNA. If I reached Cindy, would she be open to the idea of spitting in a tube?

Ashley,

I emailed you via Ancestry, but see you don't access it often. Will you please ask your mom to get in touch with me. Tel: 111 111-1111

Thanks, Peggy

Ashley's Facebook page was filled with photos and messages from friends—I had high hopes that she looked at her site every day. I had no doubt that Ashley would pass on my message. What I wasn't sure of was whether her mom would be curious and open enough to call.

Luck was on my side. The very next day, Ashley's mother, Cindy, called. As I suspected, Ashley didn't mind being contacted. Either she hadn't seen the emails from Ancestry.com or they seemed unimportant, while messages received on Facebook deserved action.

After saying who she was, Cindy began speaking without demanding to know who I was or what I wanted. She immediately launched into the reason Ashley had her DNA tested, which gave me the impression Cindy assumed my interest was in Ashley's father: "Ashley's dad was adopted, and we think his mother was Native American, who had other children." She continued on about what they did and didn't know about his family, hardly taking a breath. I finally interrupted: "Is the James Koller in Ashley's tree your father?"

"Yes," she replied.

"I think he is my father." I was stunned as soon as the sentence left my mouth—there was no "perhaps" or "maybe" included.

"Oh, I know, you must be the baby on the mantle! There was a picture, but nobody knew who it was or talked about it," she exclaimed.

I assured her that the photograph in her grandmother's house in Harrisburg wasn't me and that James would not have known about me.

During our conversation, Cindy explained she was visiting a friend in Tennessee and would call again as soon as she returned home in a day or two. She seemed eager to send photographs to me and share information from a letter that

Mark the Alive "Living," the Dead "Deceased"

Ashley, my mystery DNA match, apparently wanted her name and photo visible to the public and overcame the Website's convention of changing the names of living people to Private. This made it relatively easy for Susan to find Ashley's Facebook page.

Those who are concerned about confidentiality will be happy to know a privacy feature is available.

When adding a person to a tree, either Living or Deceased must be ticked, but usually the form is pre-ticked, based on the age of recently added people.

If "Living" is ticked, the place for a death date is not present, and the privacy feature is activated. Someone viewing the tree sees the word Private instead of the person's name.

If "Deceased" is ticked, there is a place for a death date, and filled in or not, the person's name is visible.

mentioned James' biological father. Though she had grown up in Illinois, Cindy lived about an hour's drive from me—another coincidence?

We ended up speaking for close to thirty minutes. Before hanging up, I broached the subject:

"Will you get your DNA tested?" Her response was quick and firm: "Yes." Ashley had bought two kits with the intention of giving one to Cindy. If she could get her hands on the kit right way, the wait for the results would still be six to eight weeks.

20

Who Are We?

AFTER talking with Cindy on the phone, I hoped Ashley would respond to my messages. I wanted her to share a link to her DNA so I could more easily distinguish family lines and identify matches. Using Facebook again, I sent a message offering to help find her paternal grandmother's family. According to Cindy, Ashley was disappointed that Native American didn't show up in her Ethnicity Estimate. I tried explaining in as few words as possible why a Native American grandmother might not show up in her percentages.

I wasn't surprised that Ashley, in her early thirties, hadn't looked into what the Ethnicity Estimate really means. When a professional colleague made the same mistake, I was. He and I were talking about my results, and he began criticizing the process, claiming his DNA results were not accurate and a waste of money. At first, I was confused and told him how much fun it was to look at the trees of the people I share DNA with and identify relatives. I said, "You're wrong about the accuracy. DNA results identify biologically related people with a high degree of accuracy until you get beyond a fourth cousin. Even then, it's 50 percent to about an 8th cousin." I pointed out that the accuracy was in the genes—you are related, not necessarily *how* you are related.

He replied, "I know my grandmother was a Native American, and it didn't show up at all."

I knew then he was talking about the Ethnicity Estimate, not his DNA matches. He made the same mistake Ashley did about her grandmother.

I said, "Grandma's DNA is in your here-and-now genes, not from thousands of years ago. I told him to think of the Ethnicity Estimate instead as being about people thousands of years ago who may have been the ancestors of *your* ancestors.

In contrast, DNA matches, Shared Ancestor Hints, DNA Circles, and Migrations are there because you and the others who have submitted tests share DNA. These are your relatives who share genes with ancestors going back seven to ten generations. Who you are—your heritage, ethnicity, culture, and race—can be found with the help of your DNA relatives.

In my message to Ashley, I added a personal note about my grandson Noah, who has Native American ancestors on his father's side. My daughter thought her husband should have marked it on the baby's birth certificate. (Birth certificates, in this day and age, still have a box for race?) I didn't mention the birth certificate idea or that my son-in-law's Ethnicity Estimate does include Native American as a small percentage.

In the census records, Noah's great-great-grandparents and their children are sometimes marked as Native American, but never by that term. The family was identified as *I* for Indian and in other years *W* for white. In some years, nothing was recorded in the Color column (choices – white, black, mulatto) for anyone. On one record "half-breed" had been squeezed into the tiny boxes.

It's amazing and wondrous regarding the adaptability of the human mind. That term in its

Ethnicity Estimates: Ancient Ancestors

The Ethnicity Estimate is about ancestors who lived thousands of years ago, not the relatives you will find in your DNA matches, nor the ancestors who belong in your family tree going back about ten generations. To obtain the percentage estimates, an analysis is done using a reference group to which your DNA has been correlated.

Ancestry.com is very open in their White Papers about the complex method used to come up with these estimates. According to the company's information, the analysis can vary depending on the day or time because of the batching process.

I think both my friend and Ashley were misled by TV spots that show peoples' reactions to receiving their Ethnicity Estimates. Someone takes off lederhosen and puts on a beret or vice versa. Focusing on these percents led people to believe that they are learning about recent ancestors—fifth- and sixth-great-grandparents, or even closer, their grandmothers.

Ancestry.com conducted a survey some time ago, asking account holders about their perceptions of the Ethnicity Estimates. I'm certainly not the only one who suggested they were misleading people into thinking *who you are* can be found in those percents rather than in your DNA matches and relatively recent genealogy.

There must have been sufficient feedback pointing out that a person's culture derives from relatively recent grandparents, your second to fifth, not to your hundredth. The TV spots seem to have altered recently, showing people not relying on their Ethnicity Estimates, but researching their DNA matches and family trees.

Shared Ancestor Hints and DNA Circles can be used to find family members and uncover more historical documents. That's how I found out most of my ancestors are German, going back to sixth- and seventh-great-grandparents.

I was learning more about the science and history of genes. According to Siddhartha Mukherjee in his book, *The Gene: An Intimate History*, our knowledge of the science of genetics increases weekly. Mukherjee says the rate of progress is such that upon publication, parts of his book would be out-of-date. This 500-page tome looked forbidding, but read like a mystery novel. I devoured every page.

In one of the comprehensive articles published by Ancestry.com, the limits of ethnicity estimation are discussed:

Ethnicity estimation is a problem that scientists around the world are still working on. We provide the most accurate estimate possible given our current dataset and knowledge of human genetics, but we're also working hard to improve the resolution and accuracy of your ethnicity estimate.

Each time we tweak our data, we automatically adjust your ethnicity estimate at no additional cost. It's possible that your ethnicity estimate will evolve along with our understanding of DNA science. (See DNA Unexpected Ethnicity Results at https://tinyurl.com/ycvfjnu9)

Detailed reports called AncestryDNA White Papers explaining the science behind DNA Matching, DNA Circles, Migrations, and Ethnicity Estimates wouldn't be everyone's cup of tea, but I love reading them. For those not as interested in what is under the hood, but how to turn the key, use the Support Center for briefer explanations.

essence (not its meaning at the time), could be said to represent a current idea: the desire to have "Native American" genes.

There seem to be many reasons why someone may desire a certain ethnicity. A friend of mine, working internationally, had no cause to believe her heritage was other than European, but hoped to find Africa listed in her Ethnicity Estimate. This was because she felt so much at home while living in various African countries.

Who am I to talk? If Holland were a specified region, I would want it in my percents. But what really counts for my genes is to find sixth-great-grandparents from the Netherlands.

21

Rendezvous

WHEN the phone rang, I was sitting at my desk, sorting DNA matches and adding records to my family tree. I shouldn't have been home. Earlier in the day, I planned to go to the gym after dinner and then to a dance. I hadn't exercised for days, but just couldn't pull myself away. These feelings and my behavior reminded me of what I've heard about addictions—every other activity pales in comparison and importance to the addictive property. And when forced away, all you do is think about it and squirm to return. The description fits.

Without much of an introduction, Cindy blurted out, "I'm fourteen miles from St. Augustine, and I have to stop for something to eat. Do you want to get together, or do you want to wait until we are sure?"

I jumped at the chance to meet Ashley's mother. She must have been on the road from Tennessee for quite a while and would have more driving ahead of her to get home. I suggested we meet at the Flying J. Eating at the truck stop just off the highway would save travel time. I was impressed when she expressed a preference for a more inviting place.

While I rushed to put on shoes, my guilty feelings about avoiding the gym disappeared, replaced with a sense of how lucky I was. Who knows how long it would be for Cindy and me to meet if I had missed her call? To make it easier for her to find the restaurant, we met at a corner gas station. We jumped out of our cars and hugged.

Settled in at Ned's, everyone's favorite local restaurant, we ordered sandwiches and beer—she drank, a good sign. She wasn't a wimp about her drive home. While we ate, I furiously took notes.

We didn't look alike. She was shorter and rounder. Because I was focused on family resemblance, she reminded me of Ronda, but that didn't make any sense—they aren't the ones suspected of being half sisters. We were immediately comfortable with each other. Anyone noticing us would assume we were old friends. She was sixty years old and worked as a special-care pediatric nurse. A nurse!

~ *MEMORY* ~

In my senior year of high school, I was accepted at the University of Pittsburgh for a bachelor of science degree in nursing. My mother thought going away to college was silly. "Why waste money when you could live at home?" As far as she was concerned, a three-year certificate program at the Polyclinic Hospital was good enough. I saved her even more money. I got pregnant, married, and moved out.

~ ~ ~ ~

I showed Cindy the information I collected from the tree hints. She confirmed Alberta was James' natural mother and that Elwood had adopted him. She didn't know anything about James' biological father and had no idea who Elberta's parents were. Cindy had met Robert and Donald, her uncles, when she was young but wasn't in touch with them. She thought they still lived in Harrisburg.

The name for James' birth father, Ward Laubach, came from a letter mailed to the family years ago. She didn't think James had kept in touch with his father or that side of the family. There was a paper plate with names from the letter which she would look for when she got home.

As soon as we were done eating, the dishes cleared, and we were on our second beer (a woman after my own heart), Cindy got out her laptop. I signed into my account and we looked at the matches Ashley and I had in common. Cindy didn't recognize any of the surnames of the matches.

Noticing a little number on the message envelope, I was thrilled to see someone had written to me. The note was from John replying to a message I had sent him. Before reading John's answer, I wanted Cindy to understand why I had gotten in touch with him. In the tree I made for James' family, the "last" hint under Alberta's Profile View showed three other public trees with a similar name. One was Ashley's. Another had an Alberta who never lived in Harrisburg. John's tree had over 11,000 people and seemed to have the right Alberta,

Until I knew for sure if James was my biological father, I probably shouldn't have been wasting my time, but I was eager to see if the DNA matches who weren't on my mother's side belonged to James' family. That meant I had to track down the correct Alberta and find *her* parents, since many matches could be second or third cousins.

The problem was that there were so many ways to spell Alberta's maiden name. Was it Karschner, Karshner, Kershner, or Kirshner? And, either there were two different women, Alberta and Elberta, who lived about the same time in the same neighborhood, or there was only one woman whose name was often incorrectly spelled.

John had three children listed for Alberta and Elwood, but all were marked "Private." James' name should have been visible since he was dead. Done with my explanation, I let Cindy read the message I sent John the evening before.

Date: January 30, 2017

John,

You and I are not showing as a DNA match, but I wonder if you will help me?

I am trying to determine if the Alberta Karschner and Elwood Koller in your tree are the parents of the James Koller I have in my tree. You have 3 private children, but James is dead, so his name should be visible. The other two should be Donald and Robert. I assume they are alive. Is this what you have?

The reason for my question is a genetic match who isn't in my family tree. James might be my surprise father.

I can't figure out how you are related to James? Your tree is so big—and I have a little screen—it's hard to follow the family lines. Has either brother or their families had their DNA tested?

Thank you, Peggy

Cindy and I, our heads close together, read John's answer.

January 31, 2017

Peggy,

Yes—you are looking at the correct Koller line. You and I would not be a DNA match since the Kollers married into my tree. My nephew Robert married Ashley, daughter of Faye, daughter of Donald, son of Elwood Koller whose wife was Alberta Mae Karschner. Their other kids were Robert and James.

I have not gotten a DNA test from Faye or Ashley, but could it be of help to you? Who is your mystery match??

John

Another Ashley? Alberta had two granddaughters named Ashley, from two sons? Another co-incidence. I began thinking of Faye's daughter as Ashley II. I wrote back on the spot.

Date: January 31, 2017

John,

WOW! I'm in a restaurant with Cindy whose father is James Koller. If you could get DNA from Faye or Ashley that would help me a lot. More when I get home and can type better.

Peggy

After hitting the send button, Cindy and I returned to our conversation about James. Her mother Louise was James' second wife. Cindy doesn't know anything about his first wife, but was sure James didn't have children with her. Louise divorced James when Cindy was about three. Rumors were that he was seeing someone where he worked. James did marry a woman he worked with who was twenty years younger, and they had a son and daughter together. Cindy confirmed what I had seen in Ashley's tree. James' third wife and their son had passed away.

Cindy didn't see James much when she was growing up. One summer, she and her mother traveled from Illinois to Harrisburg and stayed with her grandmother Alberta. Cindy said, "She wasn't warm, but gruff and a bit scary."

~ *MEMORY* ~

My grandma lived a short fifteen-minute drive from us, on Devonshire Road in a house my grandfather and uncle had built. During the summer, I often visited and stayed overnight, either by myself or with cousins. We would sit in rocking chairs on the back porch after dinner and shell peas, which had been picked earlier in the day from the big backyard garden.

Grandma was easy to be around and I know we talked, though the only thing I remember her saying was "Shit!" This happened the time she threw her cup across the table because she saw a worm in it. One of her sons, maybe it was Daddy, had stuck a rubber worm, the kind that wriggle in hot liquid, in her tea.

~ ~ ~ ~

As Cindy spoke about her parents, I realized her mother was still alive. I was surprised until I realized my mistake in thinking Louise had been born about the same time as my mother. Louise was eighty-three years old and lived in Arizona. My mother was almost eighty-three when she died fourteen years ago. I hoped Cindy would have her mother much longer. Maybe I would get to meet her one day if she came to Florida to visit Cindy.

I didn't broach the subject with Cindy, but thought: Louise is the one I would love to have a conversation with, to hear more about James. Knowing the impression I would have of Daddy if I heard about him from my mother on one of her

Peggy & Cindy

complaining days did give me pause.

Before we left the restaurant, Cindy brought up the subject of the two kits that Ashley had bought, originally wanting her mother to use one. Ashley had married a few months before and was now pregnant and moody. (Weren't we all.) Cindy decided: "If Ashley wants to keep the kit for her husband, then I'm going to buy one right away." I was glad she sounded adamant about being tested.

Walking in the door after my evening with Cindy, I looked at the family photos on the shelf above my desk in a whole new way. What if Cindy is as much my sister—biologically—as Ronda and Diane? I feel like I'm in a movie—if someone were shooting scenes of my discoveries and reactions, they could be edited for the Independent Lens documentary series on PBS.

22

Obsession, Not Addiction

Two days after our rendezvous, I received a five-word email from Cindy: "The kit has been sent." I was so excited. Another PBS show came to mind: *Finding Your Roots with Henry Louis Gates, Jr.* After researching the genealogy of a famous guest, the producers looked for a descendant willing to submit to a DNA test to confirm a newly–found ancestor, usually a grandfather or great-great-grandmother. Cindy was doing this for me—submitting her DNA to determine whether I'm a descendant of James B. Koller. The results wouldn't appear until mid-March at the earliest.

I had followed up on my short email to John, with a long explanation about what I knew about James' family history, including his adoption. I explained who my genetic match was—James' granddaughter Ashley—and practically begged him to test his niece-in-law Ashley II. Sharing DNA with Cindy would verify James as my biological father. Ashley II was the granddaughter of James' half brother Donald. Sharing DNA with her would prove that Alberta, not one of her siblings, was James' mother.

I was getting used to John's quick replies.

Date: February 1, 1917

Peggy,

I haven't done any DNA testing on the Koller side. I next see Ashley the last week of June. I will get her DNA then.

To answer your earlier question, my mother who is 90 now, has always loved ancestry, this is our common hobby now. DNA has really opened up some dead ends we had for 50 years. We have actually been able to jump over a missing ancestor. And there have been a few surprises like yours. Always something fun to research.

John

June was five long months away, and the laboratory could take up to two months to return the results! There was plenty to do in the meantime. I was determined to find James' biological father. Some of my shared matches certainly were from that family line. I sent out more and more messages: "We share DNA. Would you be willing to help figure out how we are related?"

The only aerobic exercise I got these days was when the tiny envelope indicated a message had arrived in my account. My heart raced and my blood pressure rose. I was so addicted, yet didn't feel anything was wrong because others I talked to or emailed with had the same problem, and they used the same word.

Before I got involved with DNA matching and genealogy, I used that word for other things: I'm addicted to dancing—went to every dance within a 50-mile radius. I'm addicted to dark chocolate—could never save part of the candy bar for another day. I'm addicted to my current boyfriend—wanted to talk or be with him constantly. Anyone who couldn't control his/her use of alcohol, drugs, or gambling would have mocked me for calling my strong interests in dance, chocolate, and a current lover an addiction.

Those sensations were nothing compared to the state of mind that developed after beginning my family tree and receiving my DNA results. This new feeling was demanding and persistent. All I wanted to do was sit in front of the computer and click.

Once a week I'm at my grandson's house when he comes home from school. He makes a beeline for his computer to play his car chase or war games. I used to grill him when he proudly showed me the digital points and objects he acquired during online games. When young, he collected bricks and trees for Minecraft. As a teenager, he switched to large guns and knives, and less upsetting, designer cars. "But they stay on the screen, nothing is mailed to you. None of it is *real*," I said. "You're using *pretend* money to buy *pretend* swords or cars."

A year ago I couldn't imagine how he felt. Now I empathize. Having to admit to Noah I understood his attraction to digital objects was humbling. I tried to justify my online activity with "You're just playing games, I'm learning. Gathering knowledge about our ancestors and their history is important." Noah reminded me he does learn history from war games. To prove it, he said, "In War World II the Allies were us and England. The Axis were Germany and Italy. Russia was on both sides, but at different times."

I have to admit he often surprises me with his understanding of certain words and concepts. When I ask, "How do you know that?" his reply might be, "They say it in the Monster Truck game."

Why does genealogical research and DNA matching so quickly turn from a casual hobby to an addiction for so many people? In the beginning, I thought it would be relaxing and fun to find out when and from which country each of my grandparents' ancestors emigrated. Perhaps I would have stayed focused, if not for this detour into a probable additional father.

My feelings hadn't changed, but the word I used to describe them did. A good friend convinced me *obsession* was the more appropriate term. Her son was addicted to drugs and alcohol. He had lost control of his mind and his life.

My obsession does affect my mind. If I'm not checking DNA matches or reading messages, I am thinking about how to organize my family groups. My day-to-day life has been affected. When I should be gone, to arrive on time for an appointment, I'm adding just one more relative to my tree. I put off other tasks and become grouchy when obligations keep me from looking at new matches.

At a monthly meeting of the St. Augustine Genealogy Society, a presenter gave a wonderful talk on a new program for synchronizing family trees. She also talked about the tricky process of staying on track while researching a family lineage. I learned that veering off course is common and picked up an insider phrase: a "shiny bauble" leads to yet another new name or strange

Noah learning from digital gaming

date, and by the end of an hour the original reason for your pursuit is lost to memory.

The presenter also used the word *addiction* to describe her behavior. Running late for a movie, as I have done, because I clicked again, then clicked once more, was bad enough. Her example took the cake. She quoted her husband hollering up the stairs, "Come now," he said, "or we'll miss the plane."

But my friend is correct. I haven't lost control of my life. We were using the wrong word. Our obsession makes us boring to those who are not "doing ancestry" and gives the impression we've lost our minds. We haven't. We're absorbed and having fun!

23

Reaching Out, Risking Rejection

THE day after I had dinner with Cindy, I searched online for a Donald Koller in Harrisburg and found a phone number. I hadn't thought of reaching out before. Now I wanted to connect—right away. Cindy hadn't told me anything new, but meeting her and hearing the names and details I had only seen on paper made the idea of a biological father seem real.

Waiting for Cindy's DNA results would mean delaying the call for more than a month, probably two. I had discovered through a Find A Grave record that Robert was already dead, and a public records birth date put Donald at eighty-three years old. Though I didn't know one way or the other if he were my uncle, the urge to call was so strong, I couldn't resist.

Hoping Donald still had his old-fashioned land line (as I did), I turned on Skype and made the call. I knew some people used caller ID to screen calls, but my cell phone plan had limited daytime minutes. I was relieved when a woman answered instead of an answering machine. I could hear noisy children in the background—could this be the right number? I gave my name and asked for Donald.

Without interrogating me, the woman said, "He's out, but will be back soon. I'll have him call you."

A few hours later, the phone rang and my caller ID let me know it was Donald Koller returning my call. After our greeting, I came straight to the point: "I think your brother James was my father."

He didn't seem surprised. I explained about my DNA matching Ashley, his niece Cindy's daughter. I repeated the information I had gathered about his family.

Donald confirmed each item. "Yes, our house was on Fifth Street. Yes, Jim lived there until he left for the war."

To make sure I was on the right track with James' family tree, I asked about their mother. Her name was Elberta, with an *E*, not an *A*, as I thought. He confirmed that her parents were Kate and Benjamin Franklin Karschner: "Yes, that's how it's spelled."

With this information, I could expand James' family tree with confidence. I was eager to see if the surnames for the parents and grandparents of Kate and B.F. would be the same as the ones found in the trees of my DNA matches.

Donald and I didn't talk long. I asked if he wanted me to call when Cindy's results arrived. Both his words and tone of voice assured me he wanted to hear from me.

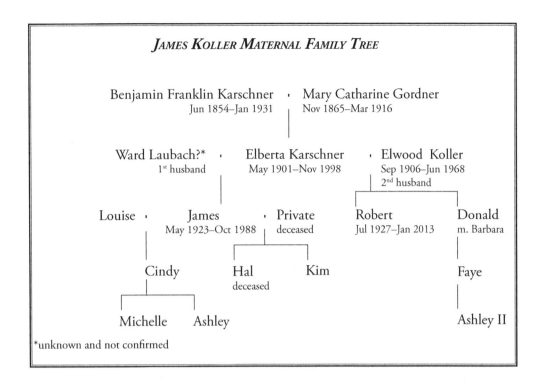

JAMES KOLLER MATERNAL FAMILY TREE

Benjamin Franklin Karschner · Mary Catharine Gordner
Jun 1854–Jan 1931   Nov 1865–Mar 1916

Ward Laubach?* · Elberta Karschner · Elwood Koller
1st husband   May 1901–Nov 1998   Sep 1906–Jun 1968
2nd husband

Louise · James · Private   Robert   Donald
May 1923–Oct 1988   deceased   Jul 1927–Jan 2013   m. Barbara

Cindy   Hal   Kim   Faye
deceased

Michelle   Ashley   Ashley II

*unknown and not confirmed

Learn More about DNA Matching

The structure of the DNA molecule was discovered in 1953 by Crick and Watson. From that time on, scientists have not stopped learning about genes and the role they play in our lives. Testing companies use massive calculations to reveal the likelihood that a match is identical by descent (IBD), by inheritance, and not identical by state (IDS), by chance. Learning about the measurement of DNA and understanding how comparisons are made between and among people are fascinating subjects.

The most challenging subject is understanding how DNA identifies relationships. Except for DNA matches of about 2500 centiMorgans (cMs) and above, which confirms a relationship of parent and child and/or full siblings, it can be difficult to determine how you are related to someone. But even in the case of parent and child, the age of the participants determines the nature of relationship, not the amount of shared genes. A viewer looking only at the amount would not be able to distinguish between parent and child.

When less than 2500 cMs are shared, doubt may play a role in determining the nature of the relationship. As the amount of shared DNA decreases, the doubt increases. For help in identifying relationships, various online sites provide cMs charts that show the range and expected average for different levels of kinship. Looking at any one chart reveals how difficult identification can be. The range for each level of kinship is not only wide (e.g., 2nd cousins 46–515), but overlaps with other groups (e.g., 3rd cousins 0–217).

Now imagine putting together a puzzle that doesn't have straight edges and four corners. This is what happens when you look at more than one chart. The ranges and averages vary, along with additional qualifiers such as intermarriage (endogamy). See page 145 for a list of resources.

PART IV Ancestors & Descendants

Contents

24

Wishing It Weren't So

Weeks had passed since I spoke with Donald. I expected any day to find out whether he was my half uncle or not. The two dates on my calendar which I had drawn red circles around—one for the arrival of Cindy's DNA and the other for Diane's—had come and gone. Instead of heading straight to the kitchen to make coffee in the morning, I signed into my account first.

In the back of my mind a debate was raging: "Maybe there was a mistake in the lab analysis and that's the reason Ronda and I aren't shown as full sisters." But that would mean there were two other errors: (1) Ashley's match with me, but not with Ronda, and (2) Bob Nicholson's match with Ronda, but not with me.

While working on my tree, I couldn't keep myself from refreshing my DNA results page every fifteen minutes or so. Just before stopping for lunch, I clicked once more and my number of matches had increased by one. Another click and there it was—Diane's name in the close family category.

I held my breath and forced myself to see how much DNA Diane shared with me. The amount—1755 cMs—meant we were half siblings. Then I looked to see the amount she shared with Ronda—2499 cMs. I don't know what I felt more, relief or resentment. Ronda and Diane are full sisters, and both Mom and Daddy are *their* biological parents.

My confidence level that my mother conceived me with another man while married to Daddy went from 99.9 percent to 99.99 percent. Maybe I was being unreasonable, but until Cindy's results arrived, I didn't want to tell anyone, even myself, that it was 100 percent certain. I was holding out … for what, I couldn't say.

I shared the news with my prospective half sister.

Date: April 17, 2017

Cindy,

I thought there was a mistake or something that could explain why Ronda was a half sister to me and why Ashley and I were matching so high. But Diane's results arrived today. She and Ronda are FULL sisters.

You sent your kit in around the same time Diane sent hers. If you match me, you won't have to tell me—I will see you in my matches!

Peggy

With so much evidence accumulated, I spent more time identifying third and fourth cousins on my paternal side. Many do confirm my DNA relationship to Elberta's parents. This doesn't necessarily prove James is my father or that Elberta is my grandmother. The cousin relationships with ancestors—especially third-great-grandparents and farther back—would be the same. What the matches did seem to "prove" was that Katie and B.F. Karschner are my great-grandparents on my paternal side.

Regardless of who my father and his mother turn out to be, I'm not my daddy's firstborn biological child. I always felt like I belonged in my family, but there were plenty of times I thought my sisters resented me—not exactly me, but something about

me. Ronda's reaction to our half sister relationship fits the pattern of their need to dismiss me. Our cousin Anne Marie (on the Nicholson side) and I never developed the habit of phone chatting, but when we do it's because I call her. When I saw her name on my caller ID, I expected bad news. In a way, it was. Ronda had sent her a one-line email: "Peggy is not a Nicholson."

25

Wild Goose Chase

MONTHS ago, once I had access to Ashley's tree, Susan seemed as eager to find James' family as I was. After she tracked down Ashley, Susan set her sights on identifying James' biological father. I joined in the search, but only after I had cut my teeth on my mother's side—DNA matches and people in trees I knew for sure were family.

We investigated and eventually eliminated the few possibilities we came across. Weeks turned into months. I checked with Cindy to see if she knew anything more than the name Ward Laubach. The only reason she knew that much was because information had been sent to James' son years ago. In her possession was an envelope with photographs and half a paper plate that had a few names written on it.

Before long, Susan and I expanded the search by considering any feasible Laubach, whether the first name was Ward or not. At one point, I was convinced a Joseph Laubach was the right man. But an email from a woman living in that part of Pennsylvania assured me he was the wrong person: "Joseph was a big man, tall and overweight, and religious. He had been happily married, so unlikely to be James' father." A happy marriage doesn't always prevent infidelity, but I took her word for it.

Susan and I had each built our own temporary trees, and I was sure I had found James' father

because the tree profile diagram "confirmed" the relationship. But there weren't any documents or shared DNA matches to support the relationship. This was a good lesson—I could make almost anyone appear to be a legitimate relative. The tree doesn't question your choices: I could find a way to make Abraham Lincoln my grandfather, and the tree diagram would "confirm" the relationship.

The software will "question" a birth date if entered for a parent who seems too young, given the child's birth date or vice versa. The warning which comes in bright red lettering can be overridden. I've seen many such mistakes in people's trees—to the point where a parent's death date was years before the child's birth date.

Strangely enough, I found a Toni Laubach among Ronda's DNA matches. This was before Diane's results came back, when I still had hope there was one paternal family for all of us. Toni responded to my inquiry, letting me know she had married into the Laubachs. Her Laubachs emigrated from Russia, though their ancestors were originally from Germany, finally ending up in Texas. None of the family, as far as she knew, had come through Pennsylvania.

From the trees of my DNA matches, I was sure James' parents, his grandparents, and generations back were from northeast of Harrisburg in the counties of Columbia, Lycoming, and Northumberland. I had been working with Jim, trying to determine who our common ancestor was. Jim had Laubachs in his tree, so I assumed that was our connection.

Date: March 28, 2016

Jim

Will you tell me how the Laubach and Hess families connect—your tree is big and I can't find where they meet.

Peggy

Sometimes it took a while to get an answer, but Jim always got back to me. After an apology for the delay, he always had good information.

Date: May 11, 2016

Peggy

Yes, the Laubach/Hess connection. I found a history lesson about them in a story. It is so very interesting as to why they are so tied together. Actually the story (as you will see) centers around 4 families, they are Hess, Cole, Laubach, and Fritz. It tells the story of how Sugarloaf township was first settled. I will find it and send it to you. It might help you and possibly make "our" connection clear.

Jim

The story of Sugarloaf was fascinating. I could spend hours reading posted stories, obituaries, and wills accessed from the Gallery link in public trees. Sometimes I came across conflicting stories of the same family. The most recent usually claimed to be the authentic story. One explanation given for the difference was that the earlier version had been adapted to be more flattering to the family.

Jim sent a copy of his tree profile diagram showing his relationship to Daisy, a third cousin once removed, who married a Laubach. Well, a Laubach by marriage was no help at all.

One of my emails to Susan shows what contortions we were going through looking for this Laubach.

Gallery in Trees

The Gallery is a place in your family tree where you can post family photos, stories, and documents. Each person in the tree has a Gallery, accessed via Profile View,

You do not need a Subscription to post personal items. Gallery items in family trees that have been shared with you can also be viewed. With a Subscription, you can peek into Galleries on public trees.

The family stories are fascinating and sometimes contradictory—a good reminder that history is what has been recorded, not necessarily what has occurred.

A male second cousin thanked me for posting a photograph he had never seen of his grandmother, surrounded by him and his cousins. Though not true in every case, females seem to be the guardians of family pictures. As the oldest daughter, I rescued the photographs my mother had saved from her mother, who was the oldest daughter in her family.

I am especially grateful when someone has attached an obituary for one of my ancestors because the information fills in gaps about those in my family tree.

Date: June 15, 2016

Susan

I put Jim and his family in my tree up to Daisy, but hadn't made her connect to me. So I went back to Jim's tree to see why I wasn't connecting—and decided to use Gordon Laubach as James' father.

Not only does Jim, his dad, and sister now show as relatives, but Horace Laubach, who I share DNA with, matches as a second cousin!

BTW, he's the uncle of the woman who has been helping me a lot, the one who voted against Joe—the large, religious Laubach.

Gordon Laubach was a good fit and I felt successful in finding the man who might be my grandfather. But he didn't appear to have children. How would I prove he was James' father if he had no descendants to whom to compare DNA? I eventually came across a tree which did show a child, and from this large, well-documented tree I had the impression that the man I wrote to was a serious genealogist.

Hello,

We are not a DNA match, but you are the only one who has a child listed for Gordon and Martha Laubach. I couldn't find anything indicating they had a child. Would you be willing to share with me where you found the documentation for the child you listed?

Thank you, Peggy

I was amazed to receive a phone call two hours later. The man's daughter had married into the Laubach family, and he was adding her husband's line to the family tree. This was the second time a non-DNA match went out of the way to help. The information about the child came from Gordon's obituary. The next day, he had generously posted the clipping to the tree. Later that same day, he called with the obituary for Gordon's child who had died the year before and was survived by five children and five grandchildren. If one of the ten were tested, would that confirm one way or the other whether Gordon was James' father?

Using the names and locations from the obituary to find a phone number would be relatively easy. Then I imagined making the phone call. When someone answered, no matter how carefully I chose my words, I would be asking, "Will you please submit to a DNA test so I can see if your grandfather had a child out of wedlock?" I wasn't prepared to take that step. Not then, anyway.

26

Sisters Galore

I hadn't been clicking to refresh my DNA screen every fifteen minutes to see if Cindy's results had been posted, because I had been out most of the day. Tapping to wake my Mac, I took a quick look. No, not yet. I put together a fast dinner, took my plate to the couch, and turned on the TV to watch *M*A*S*H*—my end of the day therapy. I figured as long as I was not confronted by the decisions Hawkeye and his companions faced, I had nothing to complain about.

The phone rang. The name on caller ID was Cindy's so I didn't hesitate to interrupt my dinner and mute the TV. She said something about an email she'd just received from Ancestry.com. They had been sending email apologies about the delay in her processing. Instead of "still processing," I heard the word "done." I jumped up, dropped my dish on the kitchen counter, and rushed to my desk. As soon as I saw the number of matches had changed from 374 to 375, my heart stood still. With another click, there she was in the Close Family category, ending all doubt.

Now I knew for sure—my paternal genes came from James Koller. After seeing his name in Ashley's

Ronda, Peggy holding Diane
Sisters I grew up with ~1953

tree months ago, I told everyone—friends, relatives, anyone I spent more than a few minutes with, "I *may* have a different father than the one who raised me."

Now I feel like I've known the truth from the moment I saw my shared matches with Ashley and the names didn't look familiar.

Before Cindy and I hung up, she told me Kim, our other half sister, and she were planning to come to St. Augustine to have dinner with me.

I couldn't wait to tell Susan and dashed off a quick, short email. She must have run to her computer after getting my note on her phone.

Date: April 15, 2017

Peggy,

OMG!!! I have been checking several times a day but hadn't logged on this evening. Well, there it is! This is so crazy even though we have known what to expect. The realization is different than the expectation. I hope you are ok with this.

Susan,

She was right—looking at Cindy's name on the screen, I felt completely different than I had while

waiting. The feeling was like a balloon releasing its air—all relaxed, no tension anymore.

Date: April 15, 2017

Susan,

"The realization is different than the expectation." I couldn't have said it better! I was amazed at the difference I felt—it seemed as if I was finding out for the first time. And it was so confirming. On the other hand it felt like I always knew—from the minute I saw Ashley's name next to yours.

I like it—I feel like I am thumbing my nose at "them" (Ronda and Diane) for how I grew up feeling like something was wrong with me. But I also feel like I have two families, which is nice.

Peggy

I don't think "Uncle" Donald doubted from my first phone call that I was his brother's daughter. Now I can call again, this time with the evidence and ask if I can meet him the next time I'm in Harrisburg.

A flurry of emails passed between Susan and me.

Date: April 16, 2017

Peggy,

That Cindy has been so welcoming is awesome. This brings tears of happiness for you.

Susan

Susan's reaction seemed to me to be more expressive than mine, and she agreed. Sharing this experience with me, though the circumstances are different, brought up memories from the years and years of wondering about her daughter. So many emotions had built up from the time she placed the baby for adoption. It was less than three years ago that they were reunited. Beth was out there, Susan just didn't know how to get to her. I had never longed for a missing family member. It seemed like one day I began with one father—Daddy—and the next day finished with an extra father.

I looked at the three names in my matches list, under Close Family: Ronda, Cindy, Diane. They were ranked by the amount of shared DNA with me. The differing amounts among the three wasn't much, but it didn't seem right that Cindy shared more with me than Diane. I felt a bit shaken, somehow cut off. Diane was my baby sister. She was four years younger, and I watched out for her, protected her. When I had a baby daughter of my own, I sometimes called her Diane by mistake because my sister was the first baby I carried around. I only met Cindy as a woman in her sixties.

But Cindy was warm and friendly. Looking at the world optimistically, what did I lose? I have four half sisters instead of two full sisters. Since 1/2 + 1/2 + 1/2 + 1/2 equals 2, I haven't lost anything. I can't help thinking of it this way, even though it might sound absurd.

Someday I may get to know these new sisters—those who share with me genes which we've inherited from our father. We can develop memories going forward, but our history can never replicate what I have with Ronda and Diane and *our* daddy. I can listen to, but not exchange, childhood stories and memories with Cindy and Kim about *their* daddy.

27

My Mother's Encounter

GROWING up, I *knew* I was the child of Margaret and Frank Nicholson. DNA results showed otherwise. Whenever I tell someone my news, I get all sorts of reactions. There are a few who immediately begin telling me about their own or a friend's surprise story. Most are curious and ask questions such as, "Didn't your father know?"

They almost always get a confused look when I answer, "No, not even my mother knew."

Disbelieving voices say something similar to, "How could your mother not know?"

"She thought her husband Nick was my father. Back then she couldn't have determined paternity, even if she suspected, which I don't think she did."

Perhaps, not in so many words, the questioner states the obvious: "So your mother was married, had sex with another man, but didn't think you could be his?"

This aspect of the situation is an irrelevant part of the birth father story for me, but fascinates others. To satisfy their curiosity, I contemplate the possibilities.

First, to set the stage:

Marg and Nick marry in March 1942.

Able-bodied men are either volunteering or being drafted to fight in World War II.

Marg & Nick
March 1942

Nick is stationed in Philadelphia, training to be a medic.

Marg, twenty-two years old, lives with her mother who owns a grocery store at 620 Kelker Street, living quarters in the rear and above.

James, nineteen, lives with his parents on Fifth Street, about two blocks away.

In November, Nick was home on furlough for Thanksgiving week.

According to his induction card, James reports for duty December 7, 1942.

Finding a reverse conception calculator online, I plugged in my birth date. I don't remember hearing that I was born earlier or later than expected. The calculator spit out: Sex likely took place between November 29th and December 5th, 1942 with conception occurring on or around December 5th. Thanksgiving was November 25th that year. The encounter must have happened after Nick returned to his outfit. I am focused on a specific encounter and don't care if there were others—I'm only interested in the one that concerns me.

To anyone who mentions an affair, I point out that it was unlikely that Marg and James could carry on a relationship without the news getting back to Nick. Harrisburg is not a big city, even now. My parents and their friends all went to the same high school and knew each other. Back then, neighborhoods were cohesive. Spending time there as a child, I remember how friendly and intimate the area felt.

Also, an affair requires more involvement, and I know from my mother's stories she was in love with Nick. Even if they had many lovers' quarrels while dating, no matter how many times they broke up, they always got back together. "He would always come to apologize. I could see him coming from far down the street. I could tell it was Nick by his walk and my heart would flutter."

They started dating in 1936, when both were sixteen years old, and married in their early twenties. After the war, they saw each other every day until he died from his second heart attack in 1986. Mom said they had been together for so long, "It's like losing one of my arms." His death didn't change her day-to-day life much because she had always taken care of their finances and the house. Mom's social life included her family if we were around, but primarily focused on shooting pool in the leagues at the American Legion and VFW. She didn't appear to suffer, but told me, "I cried every day for eight months."

When and how could this magical encounter between my mother and James have taken place?

My mother loved to dance. I don't know if James was a dancer. Perhaps they happened to dance together one night and shared a beer … and another beer. But then, what? Where could they go? I don't know when my mother bought her Studebaker. Did James have a car—a teenager about to go off to war? With neither of them having their own place, they would have had to plan and conspire. For my mother, a feeling of spontaneity would have been necessary to eliminate a sense of responsibility and reduce feelings of guilt.

There were occasions when a spontaneous tryst could have occurred. My mother told me about the "brownouts" they had during the war. These were drills with dimmed lights and shades drawn to be ready in case of German bombers. Blackouts were different—no light could be visible. The air raid siren blared and everyone had to run indoors and pull the blinds. Mom made the drills sound like preparation for a party: "We had so much fun. The siren would go off, and a group of us coming home from a movie or a dance would run in the store and have to wait until the all-clear signal came."

I knew back then young people could be out at all hours. There was never an issue of safety. People walked the streets, day or night. Doors were rarely locked. James' brother, who was only ten at that time, told me, "I knew the neighborhood like the back of my hand. On the corner of Sixth and Kelker was a bar. James hung out there a lot." James would have been underage, but I doubt local taverns were strict when their patrons would soon be off to war. Perhaps James was leaving the bar when a siren rang and joined Marg's group as they ran into the store.

When the "all-clear" sounded, James may have stayed after the others left. Or perhaps he met up with Marg when she was walking home alone and invited himself in. Maybe there was some flirting and something that began innocently went too far. (Louise, James' second wife, referring to his courtship of her, said something like, "Going after what he wanted.")

Now, to watch the play:

Marg and James are sitting side by side on the davenport, in the living room in back of the store.

James knows in a few days he will be in the army.

The dialogue begins: "Marg. Next week I'm going to war. They'll send me overseas. You may be the last woman I get to kiss before I'm killed."

Maybe Marg is agreeable:

Because she believes she's pregnant from Nick's furlough.

Because she thinks James will withdraw, a popular, though flawed, birth control method.

There are other less desirable versions:

Maybe at a certain point, she resists, but he doesn't stop.

Maybe he was never welcome in the first place.

1716 N 5th St <--> 620 Kelker St

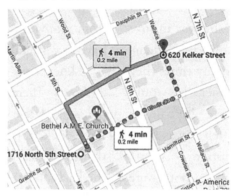

Have I covered all the possibilities? If not, these efforts to satisfy the curiosity of others will have to do. This aspect of having a biological father holds little interest for me. Yes, I would read a letter or a diary that revealed the time, place, and circumstances of the encounter. Or if those involved could tell me what happened, I would listen. But they can't, they are all dead. So I don't think about it.

More than a year has passed since the play was written. Feelings of pride about my genetic find eventually replaced those of disbelief. I'm content now with the closing scene:

"You may be the last woman I get to kiss."

I like to think of Marg, my mother, contributing to the war effort by bolstering the morale of a young soon-to-be soldier.

28

You Are the Uncle!

WITH proof that Cindy and I are half sisters, I had an excuse to call Donald again. Adapting the phrase Maury Povich uses on his TV show, I thought about announcing, "You are the uncle!"

Donald sounded pleased with the news, which gave me the courage to bring up James' biological father. "Is Ward Laubach the name of James' father?"

His lukewarm mumble, "That doesn't sound right," left me wondering if he were being truthful.

On the other hand, maybe he didn't even know the name. After all, he was ten years younger than James. Maybe the adults never talked about it. I was sure if Donald knew, he would eventually tell me.

My perception that Donald wanted to stay in touch was proved true the following day. Checking messages after a day of errands, I heard Donald's lilting, special tone of voice greeting me. "Peggy, this is your long-lost (long, breathy sigh) … aaahh, what do I call myself … your father's brother? (light laughter) to put it in simple terms. I have some questions for you and I'll call you back … at a little later date." (I couldn't bear to lose the message so moved it to a cassette.)

I called back immediately. Donald wanted to know, "Was that Martin's grocery store on Kelker Street and did you live out on Lockwillow Road?" That he was sufficiently interested to follow up

on what we talked about seemed amazing to me. I asked if he remembered seeing my mom at the store, but he didn't.

Mustering even more courage, I asked, "Could I have more half siblings who don't know James was their father?" Donald didn't hesitate. "Yes, there probably are, but I don't know how you'd find them. My brother didn't practice safe sex!"

I felt so warm toward him. I couldn't wait to meet "Uncle" Donald. My thoughts turned toward a trip to Harrisburg.

29

Discovering a Goose Egg

A half year had passed since Susan and I began the search for "Grandfather" Ward Laubach. I had located descendants of a likely candidate. Working up the courage to call a Laubach grandchild to request a DNA test seemed ridiculous, if not downright rude.

Why did it seem so important to find him, this genetic grandfather? All this thinking about a paternal grandfather brought up memories of my real grandpa, Daddy's father, Frank Andrew Nicholson Sr.

~ MEMORY ~

The term "paternal grandfather" seems too formal for the working-class family I grew up in. From the time I was little, I spent lots of time with Grandpa and Grandma. On every holiday the Nicholson family got together for dinner, and we had picnics in the summer.

Grandpa didn't die until 1961, the year I graduated from high school, but I only remember him physically from photos. My favorite is my grandparents sitting side by side in folding chairs at a family reunion, looking just like grandparents are

supposed to—the way people in their mid-sixties looked back then—elderly. He rather slender, legs crossed; she plump in a stretched-out sweater. This was one of the many pictures I chose for the family tree photo book I made for my grandson. This book, which I can barely get Noah to pay attention to except for the pages that include him with relatives, brings alive wonderful memories for me.

At first, my feelings were hurt. The family tree book took me so much time and effort. Then I realized all Noah sees are two rather old, frumpy, nondescript people. When I look at Grandma and

Grandpa & Grandma Nicholson

Grandpa, I see my cousin Anne Marie and me jolting up from our pillows in the double bed across the hall from their bedroom in the house they built themselves. We are screaming at the top of our lungs. Grandpa had snuck in, crawled under the bed, and pushed up on the coil-spring and mattress.

I look at the photo again, and I see myself sitting between them in the front seat of a 1945 Buick, careful to keep my little legs toward my grandma so they aren't in the way when my grandpa reaches for the floor shift. In the next memory, I am a bit older, a preteen, when they took me to see Gorgeous George wrestle at the Hershey Park Stadium. The arena was bigger and noisier than anything I had previously experienced. The golden robe that George wore looked shiny and slippery, and when my quiet grandpa stood and cheered, waving his arms about, I felt part of something special.

~ ~ ~ ~

Maybe I was better off forgetting about the Ward Laubach branch of my biological family tree. I was busy enough filling in the other branches and trying to identify my cousins. Once I was sure I had the correct Elberta Karschner and her parents, that part of my tree grew by leaps and bounds. I was getting much better at discerning what documents pertained to which people. I was no longer ending up with contradictory records assigned to closely related families who lived in close proximity.

I would not have guessed that it could be so much fun interacting with strangers. We behaved as if the fifty cMs of shared DNA which made us fifth cousins really meant something. With all the emails between these strangers/relatives and me, along with the voluminous back-and-forth flow of messages with Susan, my inbox was overflowing. I couldn't keep track of my leads anymore. It was time to take a break from contacting people and delete or assign labels to the emails in my inbox.

My Biological Grandfather

Ward ~~Laubach~~ Ikeler
|
James
|
Peggy

When I registered with Ancestry.com I had created a separate email account to use only for ancestry-related contacts. Gmail's labeling system is superior to folders for organizing messages. Sorting through, I came across a note from one of my matches who suggested getting in touch with Joyce, a mutual cousin, because she knew a lot about the family history. I knew Joyce and I were fourth cousins once removed through Elberta's mother's family. Since I knew who she was, I almost hit delete, but changed my mind and sent off a quick email explaining about the surprise father.

My phone number is included automatically with my signature, but I rarely get calls. Joyce was one of the exceptions. She listened patiently to my story about finding out James was my birth father. But as soon as the words, "I'm looking for his father," were out of my mouth she said, *Ikeler.* The penny dropped!

This was one of two strange names Cindy had given me over the phone a day or so after we met for dinner. She said she was reading the names from a paper plate. I had written "ikeler" because she said it was a small *i*. I made her repeat the spelling to be sure I heard her correctly. She also said something about ancestry, so I assumed they were usernames on Ancestry.com. I couldn't find anything in the member directory. That was five months before Joyce's call.

After hanging up, I changed the surname for James' father from Laubach to Ikeler. Tree hints began popping up. About the same time, Joyce inundated me with information by email.

Date: June 23, 2017

Peggy

We know in the 1923 & 24 Harrisburg city directories, Ward and Alberta were living together. Wished we could find them in 1920.

Ikeler Ward P (Alberta) auto mech Black's Garage r2253 Jefferson

Joyce

A marriage certificate would prove James' parents were married, but at least the city directory

Tossed Salad, Not Pureed Soup

The hardest thing to keep in mind is that DNA is not passed down equally from ancestors to their descendants. Children from the same parents will not have inherited the same pattern of genes, and the genes each receives from the four grandparents are likely to vary even more. The more distant a common ancestor is from a set of descendants, the more the genetic pattern will differ. In other words, siblings can be biologically related to a relative in exactly the same way, but not have inherited the same genes. In fact, one sibling may not have inherited any genes at all from a distant great-grandparent.

During my early months of genealogical research, I gave a dinner party and was explaining to my guests what I was learning about DNA. (The dinner was just for fun, but I spoke of little else at that time.) As the tossed salad was passed around, I came upon the perfect metaphor for describing genetic inheritance. The seven guests had finished eating the delicious sweet potato-ginger soup served for the first course. Each guest had received an equal share of the ingredients used to make the pureed soup. As each guest filled a salad bowl, I could point out how varied their salads were compared to the soup. One person's bowl seemed to overflow with cherry tomatoes, another dug deep and collected the walnuts that had sunk to the bottom, and a third didn't get any olives.

Among close relatives, the relatively high percent of shared DNA among family members usually won't cause consternation. Their salads will somewhat resemble each other. In more distant relationships someone in a family can be left without cherry tomatoes.

My real-life example happened with a DNA Match named Jim, his siblings, and their father, Rohr. (I first "met" Jim when he kindly answered one of my early desperate pleas for help in identifying relatives. I had mistakenly assumed he and I were related through the Laubachs. Once I had the right name—Ikeler—in my tree, I was able to find our MRCA, our common ancestors.) Jim and I share fourth-great-grandparents, Elizabeth Hixon and Samuel Kitchen. We are fifth cousins, while Jim's father and I are fourth cousins once removed.

All three of Jim's siblings had been tested, and I couldn't understand why his brother didn't show up in my shared matches with Jim. When using the Shared Matches feature, be aware that Ancestry.com sets a minimum cut off for showing triangulated relationships. Maybe Lonnie did get Kitchen-Hixon genes, but an amount too small for the software's filter.

I suggested Jim upload his family's DNA onto GEDmatch.com, a free website. He did. I could see that Jill, Jim, Laurie, and Lonnie are Rohr's children and that they share the same mother. (Her DNA is uploaded too.) Using a chromosome browser, the shared Kitchen-Hixon genes were on chromosome 10. (Mostly, I'm using ordinary language, not scientific terminology in my explanations.) Lonnie's salad bowl got only one walnut. Was it a smidgen of the family genes or could it have gotten there by chance, not by descent?

Unless you and the people you are comparing DNA with plan to use GEDmatch.com, the best way to somewhat overcome this issue with Ancestry.com's software is to share links to each other's DNA. This allows you to view another's matches directly which will show lower cMs amounts. The chart from GEDmatch.com shows how detailed their comparisons can be.

GEDmatch.com
Showing shared DNA
(centiMorgans)
among matches

GEDmatch	Peggy	Rohr-parent	Jill	Jim	Laurie	Lonnie
Peggy		50	22	44	50	6
Rohr-parent	50		3567	3570	3573	3572
Jill	22	3567		2664	2699	2774
Jim	44	3570	2664		2597	2805
Laurie	50	3573	2699	2597		2774
Lonnie	6	3572	2774	2805	2774	

GEDmatch.com

GEDmatch.com, a free website with additional features available at a low cost, accepts uploads of DNA from testing companies such as Ancestry.com, 23andme, and FTDNA. Instructions are on the GEDmatch.com site. Some might consider the openness of this site a disadvantage, but others, like myself, like the advantages.

- You can see DNA matches with people who tested with other companies.
- You can easily and quickly see how many centi-Morgans (cMs) you share with all your matches. (On Ancestry.com you must look at each match one at a time.)
- Not only can you see on which chromosomes you and a relative share DNA, but also which segments match on any one chromosome.
- The amount of cMs is transparent among all shared matches. (On Ancestry.com, you cannot see how much DNA two of your matches share with each other, unless one of them has shared his/her DNA link with you,
- Personal emails allow direct contact between matches.
- Helpful tools for various ways of viewing relationships among matches are available.

showed them living together the year he was born, as well as the following year. In the 1928 directory, Ward was listed alone, still working as an auto mechanic at Black's Garage. After seeing how useful city directories could be, I began paying more attention to them. By ten o'clock that evening, Joyce had sent family group sheets of the Ikeler family, dating back to the early 1800s.

DNA led me to a biological father James Koller. Genealogical records confirmed Elberta Karschner was his mother, and Catherine "Katie" Gordner and Benjamin Franklin Karschner were his maternal grandparents. Ward Ikeler was finally identified as James' biological father. Ward's parents were Minnie Crawford and Boyd Ikeler, With many cousins from all four lines sharing DNA with me, there is no doubt my "paternal genes" are inherited from the Karschner-Gordner and Ikeler-Crawford families.

When I first heard the last name of my biological grandfather, I was glad the issue was settled. More meaningful were the happy memories about Grandpa Nicholson the search had brought up. Someday I would probably see a photo of Ward Ikeler. Because there are no memories, I expected my feeling would be similar to Noah's when he looked at his photo book of dead ancestors: "So what?"

Noah's Book

30

Quirky Death Certificates

DEATH certificates are good sources of information if they are complete, written legibly, and the information is correct. Sad to say, this is rarely the case. Depending upon the state, complete certificates will have the birth and death dates of the deceased, his or her parents' names, including the mother's maiden name. Other important details are the address of the deceased at the time of death, length of time residing there, and where the death occurred if not at home.

Obituaries are even more unreliable. They can vary from as little as name and date of death to a full account of the person's life. The most useful give the names of both living and predeceased spouse(s) and children, as well as siblings, of the deceased. I was frustrated by the irritating habit of listing a deceased person's sister by her husband's name, such as Mrs. Jacob Garman. Why couldn't she at least have her own first name!

Reading over the documents for the objective content was easy. Absorbing the details as they related to a specific person made me feel happy or sad. A person can have lived "all his life" at one address and died peacefully at home. The length of time was spelled out—89 years, 2 months, 4 days. A good long life. In other cases, life was much too short—2 years, 3 months, 28 days.

What came as a shock was how often I smiled or even laughed out loud at some of the death certificates. The deaths themselves weren't funny, just the phrasing used by the attending physicians. Or a physician was called too late: "He was dead when I arrived."

My favorite showed up with the Garman family, my maternal grandfather's line. I had added John Garman and his wife to my tree and hoped to find his parents. Luckily, they were named on his death certificate. I was making progress. I couldn't believe my eyes when I saw John's cause of death in very neat handwriting:

"Must have been some heart condition which developed suddenly."

The physician's handwriting on Samuel F. Garman's death certificate was also easy to read. The death occurred at 7:05 a.m. on July 2, 1921, age noted as 69 years, 5 months, 20 days. The cause of death was set down in three lines:

fracture of base of skull
struck by railway train
accidental

That's all I would have known, except for an attached news clipping from the *Patriot News*.

The crash … between an eastbound freight and a motor work car on the Pennsylvania Railroad resulted in the deaths of four persons and injuring of three others.

The Harrisburg newspaper reported the names and ages of the others, but Samuel was granted special notice.

Samuel Garman, one of the victims, was employed by the railroad for many years and would have gone on the pension list in another month. He was 70 years old and well known to railroaders in this city.

I've yet to figure out how I'm related to Samuel. He's in my tree, along with his wife and children, none of whom are connected to any branch that leads back to me. As a result there is no designation under his name for our relationship. Someday I expect to open a document and find a sibling or spouse that solves the mystery. Though I suppose not every Garman in Dauphin and the surrounding counties has to be related to me.

Disappointingly, there were no attached articles to provide more information about these death certificates of cousins from my biological father's family:

Cordelia Hayman, first cousin twice removed, née Schultz, a housewife born March 5, 1880 and died June 22, 1937 at "57y 3m 17d." The cause of death was suicide by 75g amytal (potent hypnotic) because of malignant arthritis.

John Oliver Stackhouse, first cousin three times removed, grandson of Kate and John Gordner, my great-grandparents, committed "suicide by drowning" in 1939, a month after he turned sixty-five years old.

Ella Mae Gordner, third cousin once removed, seventeen years old, died from a fractured skull as a result of an automobile accident on Route 254. The interval between the "onset of the disease or condition directly leading to death" was two days and three hours.

Strangulation by hanging was the immediate cause of death for Betty Maxine Gordner, third cousin once removed, age twenty-six. "Self-induced" was squeezed in above the word "hanging." Was this to clarify the act was not perpetrated on her? The condition was due to "Mental Disturbance, for the last three months." Onset to death took thirty minutes.

Because the deaths happened long ago and seemed remote, the descriptions were intriguing and entertaining at first. Then it hit me. Suicide is often the result of depression. Even today, with the advances in brain biology and modern medications, people suffer without relief. How many

generations are included in the study of inheritable diseases?

On the Nicholson portion of the tree, I was adding one of my great-aunts and came across a tree hint for her husband Clarence. For one person, the Find A Grave site may have almost nothing recorded, while for another, there is an extensive obituary. I was hoping to get the uncle's birth date and confirm the name of their child, but only his parents and eight siblings were listed. His wife and child were not mentioned.

Just as I was about to exit the site—finally following Susan's lead not to add unnecessary people to the tree—my attention was drawn to the only sentence on the page. "Died by judicial electrocution for murder of George Bushman." A photo of the tombstone showed the birth and death dates of Clarence and his parents. He was born in 1900 and executed in 1921. Adding to the sadness of a young death was the date of his mother's death, 1944. I can imagine how awful this was for her. A saying came to me for this experience: It's against nature for a mother to bury a child.

Switching to my mother's side of the family—my fifth-great-uncle Abraham Brinser was seen by a physician on May 23, 1910, and died less than a month later, on June 15 at 5:30 p.m. The cause of death was listed as "softening of the brain" which lasted thirty days, with "would not eat" listed as contributory for eight days. Abraham was eighty-three years old and died at home.

At ninety-two, Aunt Doris had softening of the brain, if that is a good phrase for dementia. It wasn't Alzheimer's. She knew who she was and who we were. Over a number of years, her quality of life decreased: first, with the loss of her driver's license, then a move from an independent living facility to a nursing home. Aunt Doris' sons, Allen, Ross, and Scott, lived nearby and continued to tease and have fun with her.

Growing up, my sisters and I each had a male cousin our own age to play with, which reduced the disappointment of not having brothers.

There came a moment, after being confronted with so many "half" relationships on my paternal side and no genetic connection with my Nicholson cousins, when I realized nothing had changed with my mother's side of the family. Aunt Doris and my cousins were related to me in exactly the same way. I liked that.

Scott, Ross, Allen
Aunt Doris' sons
Martin First Cousins 2012

The last time I saw Aunt Doris, we ate lunch in the nursing home because her legs weren't strong enough to get into her son's car. She wasn't eating much and only enjoyed ice cream.

Dementia was often listed on death certificates as the cause of death. I thought this must be an old-fashioned term used by physicians for older people who didn't die from an obvious disease. With a little research, I learned there are multiple forms of dementia that take different paths, similar to cancer's variations. In the end, most people with late-stage dementia die of a medical complication related to their underlying dementia, such as an infection or blood clot. The immediate cause of death may be a medical complication, but it is the dementia that predisposed and made the person too weak to recover. One site was explicit: "Dementia itself is fatal. At times this is appropriately listed as the cause of death on a death certificate, as late-stage dementia is a terminal illness."

Toward the end, she looked tired and ready to die. I felt sad when they treated Aunt Doris' pneumonia with antibiotics, simply to keep her alive when she seemed so near to letting go of this world. Besides dementia, I often saw pneumonia listed on death certificates. Over one hundred years ago Sir William Osler, the father of modern medicine, referred to pneumonia as "the old man's friend" because it is a swift, relatively painless way to die. I suppose only swift and relative to worse ways because, from what I read, a person feels like they are drowning. Osler died of pneumonia.

Writing about death reminded me of the moment I learned the name of my biological father and simultaneously saw he was no longer alive. This didn't surprise me, because the daddy who raised me was also dead. He died in bed from a second heart attack. I don't know exactly what was written on my bio-father's death certificate. What will mine say?

31

Family Inheritance: Nature ~~versus~~ & Nurture

JAMES suffered from colon cancer. This is my least favorite thing about him. Cancer contributed to my mother's death, so learning about his didn't create a new worry, only added to it. Mom also had heart issues caused by a floppy valve and high blood pressure, neither of which plague me. Though no longer relevant for my health, Daddy's heart problem appeared to result from lifestyle choices—he worked hard, smoked, and drank. After he died, Mom told me he had stopped taking his heart medication: "Your daddy didn't like how the pills made him feel." Her openness had no bounds: "They took away his sexy feelings."

After learning about James, I had to correct my medical history. I've never had a mammogram—too much radiation and too many false negatives. Exposure to X-rays is diagnostic, not preventative like a colonoscopy. There are risks, but I've always been religious about following the recommended screening periods. Last year the gastroenterologist told me routine screenings were stopped at about seventy years of age. As one ages, the risks associated with a colonoscopy outweigh the normally slow growth of cancer—the person is more likely to die of something else. Because I'm in such good health, the physician recommended staying with the five-year interval. With my newly discovered medical history, I'm more than willing to do so.

When I spoke with my daughter about the physician's recommendation, Sherry reminded me that she and my grandson also have a new medical history. I didn't say it out loud, but wondered: Would knowing more family history have made a difference in my son's life?

Family medical histories contribute to our understanding of which diseases, physical and mental, are more likely to be inheritable. How reliable can these studies be if the data supplied, unknowingly, may have come from the wrong family of origin? In my case, I had given the wrong medical history for the paternal side of my family.

The up-to-date scientific research has replaced the nature *versus* nurture controversy with nature *interacts* with nurture. This concept of nurture—meaning environment—refers to much more than, "Growing up, did you get enough love?" Epigenetics, a new field of research, is about how the environment—diet, exercise, and stress—influences genetic expression after birth. Even before birth, environment affects our genes. Identical twins may have gotten their start with the same genes, but how these twin genes will function in two babies—two environments—is not identical. *Scientific American*, in an April 3, 2008 online post, made this point in the title of an article: "Identical Twins' Genes Are Not Identical."

In the past year, I've read a lot about how nature and nurture work together to produce many of our traits. Isolating biological causes from complex environments for human beings is close to impossible. Can this also be true for isolating environmental causes? In a chapter in *The Tipping Point*, Malcolm Gladwell made the case that a rash of suicides in a geographic area could be understood as an epidemic.

I understand James' son, Hal, after serving for six years, left the armed service for emotional reasons. Maybe I'm wrong, my details are sketchy, but he likely suffered from a bipolar disorder. For a while in his late twenties, my son, Michael, received disability payments based on a psychiatric diagnosis. His behavior showed all the signs of bipolar depression, which at one time was called manic-depression.

Hal, forty years old, chose suicide. Michael, ten years later, just months from his fiftieth birthday, chose the same way to end his life.

Michael was intelligent and had overcome the debilitating part of his illness that had previously kept him from a successful career and full social life. I had stopped thinking anything bad was going to happen. The unconscious recklessness, a terrible motorcycle accident, and deliberate attempts at harm, from which he allowed himself to be rescued, had stopped long ago.

If collecting correct medical histories will lead to cures, or at least better treatment for inheritable diseases, let the record show that James' son and grandson may have suffered from a similar illness. These creative, bright young men didn't find the help they needed to live their three score and ten.

Generous Genealogists

I have received an embarrassment of riches that helped ease me through genealogical labyrinths. Many people who have done the painstaking work of researching the family genealogy would enjoy sharing what they have learned. Here are examples of how I came to be offered materials.

I arranged a surprise mini-reunion for my mother and Aunt Doris with three of their first cousins. The cousins, grandchildren of Gertrude and Edward Briner, hadn't seen each other in years. We gathered for lunch at Mom's house on Lockwillow Avenue in Harrisburg. I had fun listening to the five of them reminisce about their adventures when young and tell stories I hadn't heard before. I wish I could remember the funny nicknames they had for each other.

My mother died a month later in February 2003. Fourteen years passed before I was obsessed with genes and genealogy. I thought one of the cousins might be able to help me.

During one of my trips to Harrisburg, Susan and I visited the only Briner cousin still alive. At 90, Bill was spry and mentally alert. (This gave me hope.) He had a book ready to show us: *Briner Family History: A Genealogy of George Michael Breiner and Anna Catharina Loy, married 1756/7 (sic) in Pennsylvania* by F.D. Myers and J.A. Clouse. Because it had been published in 1984, there were many names I recognized, including my own. I was pleased to see my children's and their father's names recorded for posterity next to mine. The Briner book was out of print, but I found digitized lists from the book online.

Susan and I should have thought about searching for books about the family lineages we share—the

Marg, Emmett, Sis, Bill, Doris January 5, 2003

Martins and the Garmans. Luckily, someone mentioned such a book to Susan: *On the Far Side of the Sea: Odenwald Ancestors of Some Early Pennsylvania Germann / Garman Families* by C. W. Garman. She ordered it and had it within two weeks. Check for similar books for your family surnames.

The first materials about the Ikelers came via email from the Joyce Ingerson who helped identify my biological paternal grandfather as Ward Ikeler. That information helped me find James' first cousins and led to more materials. When I visited with Donna Ikeler Laubach, she pulled one document or photo after another out of her archives. I went home loaded up. She mailed more things to my home including *The Ikelers: A Family Chronical 1753-2018* recently completed by Albert Ikeler.

Make an effort to call and visit older relatives no matter the distance—you may find big-hearted cousins as I did.

The branch of my tree that needed the most work (excluding the one extending from Simon Martin) stemmed from the father of my biological grandmother, the Karschners. There were few DNA matches, but finally I received a response to one of my messages. Mary and I made an appointment for a phone conversation. We determined we were fourth cousins. Our common ancestor was our third-great-grandfather Michael Karschner born in 1799. Mary had been doing genealogy for years. The next thing I knew she was asking for my address. Within a week I received printed materials and a DVD.

I've developed a stereotype about genealogists—they are generous people.

Part V Creating Connections

Contents

32

DNA Corroborates Genealogy

ONE day the name Mike Bangs appeared in my 3rd cousin category. Our shared matches included Cindy and Ashley, which meant our relationship was on my paternal side. Depending upon his age, our common ancestor would probably be a great- or great-great-grandparent. If he had information, at least back to his grandparents, our relationship should be easy to find.

Bangs was not a name I had come across previously, nor did Mike have a family tree which could point me in the right direction. My shared matches with him were different from those I had identified as belonging to James' mother Elberta. My tree was full of her ancestors. I had recently found the right name for James' father, but the branches on Ward Ikeler's part of my tree were still sparse. I was so excited because I hadn't yet confirmed a DNA match on the Ikeler side.

In my first contact with a close relative, I hesitated to bring up my unusual relationship to the family. With more distant cousins, I usually mentioned finding a "birth" father. It is unlikely they had contact with the family members involved, and my openness seemed to bring out a desire in others to be helpful. Often in a return message, there was an interesting story about their own or a friend's unexpected results. My message to Mike was noncommittal about how I might be related to him.

Date: July 7, 2017

Subject: Ikeler relationship?

Mike

You popped up today as my closest third cousin. Our shared matches show we are related on the paternal side of my family and more likely through the paternal grandfather Ward Ikeler. Will you have a look at my tree and let me know if you see how we are related?

Peggy

While waiting to hear from Mike, I added Ikeler relatives to my tree. Locating a Bangs was the key. The surname of a son is straightforward and immediate. A daughter's surname is another story. Unless she never married, her husband's surname has to be located. This is dependent upon finding a marriage certificate, an obituary for the parent, or maybe a census record that includes a son-in-law. Instead of *birth* name, Ancestry.com uses the term *maiden,* which sticks in my throat.

~ *MEMORY* ~

My college education and feminist awakening began in lockstep in the early 1970s. My perspective on a woman's role in the family and world altered as I began to notice the subservient position the legal system enforced on us. I came to dislike *maiden,* a way to refer to the surname a woman is born with—as though every young maid will become Mrs. Someone Else! About to finish a master's program in 1976 and start a new job where no one knew me, I decided to reclaim my birth name.

Waiting for the perfect moment—a good meal with plenty of wine—I told my husband about my intentions. Pointing out how unfair taking on someone else's name was for a woman seemed to win him over. The marriage ended a few months later. He was a second husband and no children were involved.

⌐ ⌐ ⌐ ⌐

Ward's two sisters and one brother were in my tree, but I hadn't gotten around to adding their parents, spouses, and children. I searched for the married names of the women, and there it was—sister Beryl had married a Bangs! I sent off a quick note to Mike, asking whether he was the son or grandson of Beryl Bangs. Either way our common ancestors were my great-grandparents Minnie and Boyd Ikeler.

I waited three long weeks for his answer. He was the grandson of Beryl, which meant we were second cousins. The lack of suspiciousness from the people I came in contact with surprised me, but Mike outdid them all. Knowing me from only two skimpy emails, his response included the names of his whole family, including the wives and children of second marriages, siblings, and his son. Along with middle names!

As soon as I learned James was adopted, I worried my biological grandfather would never be known. I had been completely satisfied with the genealogical evidence, but finding genetics to corroborate the paper trail was delicious!

I was reminded that the half-year-long wait about Elberta, my biological grandmother, was coming to an end. John (who planned to collect DNA from Ashley II) and I had exchanged emails for a few weeks after our first contact. Then months went by without a word from him.

James had lived with his aunt Sarah for more than a year when he was very young. Was she his mother? Elberta had three brothers. Maybe James was the result of one of their youthful indiscretions.

I emailed John to ask if the DNA results were back yet. Two weeks later, without bothering to change the subject heading, I had my answer—short and sweet.

Date: July 26, 2017
RE: Ashley II's DNA?
Ashley DNA is back. You match.
John

I looked at my DNA matches immediately. Ashley II, Donald's granddaughter, shares 260 cMs with

---

Boyd A. Ikeler · Minnie C. Crawford
surprise paternal great-grandparents
MRCA

Ward grandfather	**Beryl** great aunt
James birth father	**Robert** 1st cousin once removed
Peggy /Cindy 1820 /Ashley 1014 /Mike 189 **Cindy** half sister /Mike 348	**Mike** 2nd cousin
Ashley half niece /Mike 176	

Note: Shared amount of DNA/cMs

Ward & Alfred

me and 249 cMs with Cindy. This confirmed that Elberta, not one of her siblings, was James' mother.

Some people may notice that shared DNA with Mike Bangs confirmed my Ikeler-Crawford great-grandparents, but didn't "prove" Ward was James' father. The genetic match to Mike would have been the same if Ward's older brother Alfred were James' father. This is correct, but the historical records and family photographs supplement the genetic evidence to my satisfaction.

James with his mother Elberta

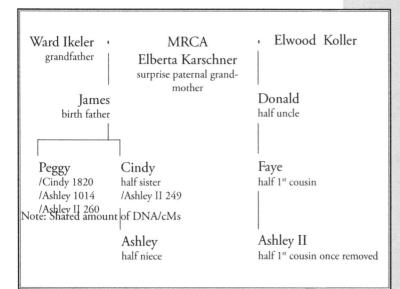

The "Final" Tree Hint

Early in my search for James' family, I came across his mother in a tree with over 15,000 people. John, the owner of the tree, did not share DNA with me, but I sent him a message anyway: "How are you related to Alberta?" (This was before I knew her name was spelled Elberta.)

It turned out that John's nephew had married Elberta's great-granddaughter Ashley. This young woman was not my Ashley. She was Donald's granddaughter. I decided to call her Ashley II.

I wish I could have thought of a better name for that one "final" hint that remains after all the others have been accepted or ignored. When this hint is opened, other family trees are revealed—sometimes one, other times twenty or more. The software assumes (based on name, dates, etc.) that the person you have in your tree is the same one in those trees, which isn't always correct.

After this experience, I made it a point to review the family trees under the "final" tree hint on a regular basis. Besides finding helpful information, the photos and stories in the Gallery are educational and entertaining.

Don't overlook these trees, even if you don't share DNA with the account holder. They can be helpful in gathering information.

When I come across names and dates that are incorrect in these trees, I have sent "correcting" messages. Sometimes I don't hear back, but usually I receive a grateful Thank You!

33

Close As I Could Get

I'LL never know James Koller. He died before I discovered he was my biological father. The closest I would get was to his brother Donald. I flew to Pennsylvania at the end of July to meet him. James, his brothers, and my mother grew up in the same neighborhood in Harrisburg. During our first phone conversation, Donald told me he had moved out of the city to rear his children. Many young couples including my parents did the same after the war and during the 1950s. Another coincidence—Donald and his wife Barbara live in Paxtonia, not two miles from where I grew up.

My rental car came with a built-in GPS which I wanted to learn to use for my out-of-town trip the next day. When I entered the Kollers' street address, what I considered incorrect directions were displayed. But that was because the surrounding area had changed so much. Houses and roads had replaced the woods, ponds, and streams of my childhood. The Kollers' house was in Pleasant Hills, not a controlled development like the planned communities of today. Pleasant Hills was a nice residential area with houses built over a span of years, each one different from the other and separated by real yards. From my house—which wasn't in any kind of development—I would walk the mile or so to Pleasant Hills to play with friends or go sledding on Curvin Drive. Nowadays most kids would expect to be driven that far. Even without the GPS, I wouldn't have trouble finding the address because one of my best school friends had lived on the same street.

～ *MEMORY* ～

Using our own rules, my friend and I could keep a Monopoly game going all weekend. We played late into the night, until her mother hollered for us to get to bed. Staying up late playing Monopoly was nothing compared to the trouble we got into when one of my friend's loafers fell off while swinging on a monkey vine over the stream. Her mom was angry because the shoes were new. She made us go out and search again, but by then it was dusk. There were certainly no people to be afraid of, but the woods in the dark! We giggled through our terror and ran back home. The loafer was never recovered.

～　～　～　～

Spotting the Kollers' address on the mailbox, I pulled into the driveway where two cars and a truck were parked. I wondered if Donald's three adult children, my "half" first cousins, were also there to meet me. Part of me hoped so—a welcoming party like you see on TV when long-lost relatives find each other. Donald was opening a sliding door where the garage door should have been. He seemed to know what I was going to ask because as the words came out of my mouth, "Do I look like him?" he vaguely shook his head no. This didn't surprise me. Cindy, James' daughter, didn't react to my looks at all.

The garage had been converted into a family room and was obviously used as the main living room. No one else was there, all three vehicles were theirs. Barb, Donald's wife, motioned me to a chair and said, "Something to drink. Coffee or a soda?"

Returning with drinks, she brought slices of zucchini bread she had made for the occasion. I immediately felt comfortable in their presence. How would I ever know if the genetic bond created my feelings for Donald or if it was because he is a nice, sweet, warm person? Knowing it's probably both, I prefer the drama of the biological connection.

Our conversation started out with the weather and then warmed up to cover many topics—the present, the past, our children, and travel. During one of our earlier conversations, Donald had given me the correct names for his mother and her parents. I wanted to know more about Elberta and her family. He didn't know much about his grandparents, Kate (Gordner) and Benjamin Franklin Karschner. From what Donald knew, Elberta had little to do with her family after she moved away at a young age to be with James' father. Donald remembers seeing his grandparents only once, when the family drove to Columbia County to visit.

I asked Donald if he would like to go with me the following day to a Gordner-Stackhouse Reunion just north of Columbia County. These were his relatives more so than mine. "We could look for the farm where Elberta grew up." He declined. Maybe someday Donald, Barb, and I will drive up and find the old Karschner homestead.

Peggy & Uncle Donald July 2017

He had gotten together a few photographs to show me. Afraid that taking a picture of Elberta and her four siblings out of the frame might cause damage, the three of us worked at getting a good copy using cell phones and my iPad. Later I uploaded the photo to my tree, hoping it would get comments from any Gordner or Karschner descendants who came across it.

My favorite part of the visit was hearing stories about James. Donald told me that when Elberta and Elwood were first together they struggled financially, so they sent James to live with her sister for a year. Donald spoke so lovingly about James but was still willing to share unflattering stories about him. James set fire to an outhouse when he was around seven. I got the impression he might have been called a juvenile delinquent.

I wondered what influence the separation of his parents might have had on James. Donald didn't know how old James was when Elberta and Ward stopped living together. From the census record, we knew that Elberta and Elwood were together by the time James was six. Donald did not think that James spent time with his biological father while growing up.

I wanted to know more: "What was he like as a person?"

"My brother was easy to get along with and full of fun. And he loved to travel. Jimmy was always going off somewhere. I didn't think he would ever settle down, but he did in Chicago—once he got married."

Donald went on to explain that he and Barb visited James and his family in Illinois and later in Florida. They were close as a family group, to the point that even after James passed away, they continued to visit his wife and children.

This contrasted with the relationship Donald had with Robert, his "full" brother. Donald still seemed upset and hurt when he explained, "Bob and his wife celebrated their fiftieth wedding anniversary, but we weren't invited. And, we didn't find out Bob died until eighteen months later."

Donald's comments reminded me that my romantic notion that shared genetic matter guarantees warm relationships was faulty.

There is a saying, "icing on the cake," which means something good gets even better. James' brother supplied the icing. I knew that James had been in the army and had served overseas during most of 1944. Donald filled in the details: "James flew from England to Normandy on D-Day and made his first jump. He was injured and was hospitalized in England." Donald took on a much graver attitude when he talked about James' involvement in the Battle of the Bulge. He said of the 750 who participated, only thirteen came back alive.

I said, "He must have been fearless."

(Later, I looked for documentation for James' participation in the Battle of the Bulge, which Donald is sure I'll find. A cursory review of the dates indicates James had returned to the US before the Battle began. More research on my part is needed.)

PVT. JAMES B. KOLLER

Pvt. James B. Koller, paratrooper, injured in the D-Day invasion of France, was invalided to England recently where he is a patient in an Army hospital. Private Koller is the son of Mr. and Mrs. Elwood Koller, 1716 North Fifth street. His wife is the former Miss Dalitha Jane Terch, of 2028 North Sixth street.

Paratrooper James injured during D-Day invasion

I had looked forward to the visit and expected to enjoy learning more about James. On the other hand, I imagined Barb and Donald may have been apprehensive about my attitude. I'm an extrovert and find meeting strangers easy and comfortable. I'm not the least bit shy. If they had been on guard, my own behavior may have changed, making conversation difficult. But the opposite happened. As the afternoon wore on, the three of us revealed more personal information about ourselves. Barb and I found we had something in common—she had also lost an adult child. Toward the end of the visit, my heart took an extra beat when Donald said, "Oh, I can see James in you." We shook hands when I arrived, but hugged hard when I left, both tearing up a little.

Karschner Siblings
Charles, Elberta, Hurley, Sara, C. Brit

34

Family Reunions

Oɴ a bright, beautiful Sunday morning, I set off for a full day of travel to meet more of James' relatives. In early afternoon, I would have lunch with at the Gordner-Stackhouse reunion with third and fourth cousins from his mother Elberta's side of the family. Later in the day, I would visit two of James' first cousins from Ward Ikeler's family. During the two-hour drive north, I thought about the reunions of my childhood, which mostly happened south, not north, of Harrisburg.

~ *MEMORY* ~

Mamie and Frank Nicholson, my paternal grandparents, the ones I grew up with, were from Gettysburg but moved to Harrisburg before their first child was born. Grandpa had graduated from Gettysburg College and was an engineer. We were told he helped build the two 145-foot-tall pylons that flank the west end of the State Street Bridge near the state capitol complex. Reading about the history of the towers, I was surprised to learn that atop each was a massive eagle weighing 300 tons, one eagle representing the US Navy, the other the US Army. Dates carved into the facing sides represent eight wars the US was involved in before World War I. How could I have grown up and lived in the area all those years and never noticed the eagles and the dates? The next time I'm in Harrisburg, the bridge will be a sightseeing stop.

Grandma's sisters stayed in Gettysburg all their lives. At a reunion on Aunt Carrie's farm, Mom "helped" with dinner: she shot a chicken. From then on, I knew the phrase "run around like a chicken with its head cut off" wasn't just a saying because I had seen it with my own eyes. Aunt Mill's farm was not far from

Nicholson-Biddle Reunions
Aunt Mill's ~1948
Doersom Airport Gettysburg (lower) ~1960

Ike's. I was always impressed that we were so close to where the president of the US had his own farm. (Carrie and Mill were, of course, my great-aunts.)

Aunt Mill - Aunt Carrie - Grandma Nicholson

Curious about how often he might have been there, I checked online. Dwight Eisenhower and his wife Mamie—same name as my grandma—bought their farm in 1950. The farm served as a weekend retreat for the president and a meeting place for world leaders. After they left the White House in 1961, the Eisenhowers made the farm their home.

⁓ ⁓ ⁓ ⁓

The Gordner-Stackhouse reunions are held every year on the last Sunday in July in Lycoming County, 85 miles northeast of Harrisburg. Grandmother Elberta's maternal great-grandparents, my third-greats, Mary Catherine Stackhouse and John Gordner, initiated the reunions. I'm sure Elberta would have gone to the reunions, at least when she lived nearby. Would James, as a baby or young child, have been taken to one? I'm not sure when she moved to Harrisburg.

After living in Florida for fourteen years, driving up high hills gave me pause, but the real mountains on the way to Unityville were intimidating. Turning left down a dirt road I found myself transported back in time into a farmyard with a big barn

in front of me and an old house to the side. The farmer, in overalls, told me to turn back to where I had come from and then bear right instead of the left I had mistakenly chosen. I did as instructed, and around the bend farther down the road was the church and cemetery. (Later, when I was leaving, someone directed me to a new macadam road. I guessed the GPS hadn't updated itself with the recently installed road.)

I parked as the others were doing, on the grass between the church and the cemetery, I climbed the hill toward the picnic pavilion. I looked for Robert Gordner, my third cousin once removed, and his wife Dotty. We were in touch, as seemed to happen with many of my DNA cousins, via a convoluted series of steps. First, I learned about the reunion in an email from a DNA match I was trying to identify.

Date: June 25, 2017

Subject: RE: How are we related?

Ms. Nicholson,

My grandmother's mother was a Stackhouse who married into the Gordner family. I am a 5th generation grandson of one Jonathon Gordner of Unityville. There are at least "4 clans of one tribe" of the Gordners in the area.

I am pastor of St. John Lutheran Church there, a.k.a. "Gordner's Church." Robin, the daughter of Dotty and Robert, our church members, is quite "up" on the Gordner family, and perhaps I can put you in touch with her.

FYI, The Gordner-Stackhouse Reunion happens every year at our church on the last Sunday in July, which would be the 30th this year. If there is something you might wish for me to announce at that reunion, please send it to me.

Sincerely,

Ron Montgomery

Next, when I wasn't able to reach Robyn, who, in addition to being the family genealogist, was also the reunion organizer, Ron gave me the number for her parents. My brief call to them satisfied me that I was welcome to attend, no matter my newly-found status as a Gordner. One to two hundred or so people usually came to the reunion. Two days later, Robert called me back and asked if I would like to sit with them. Though I should have been used to it by now, the receptiveness of people I met because of my little test sometimes brought tears to my eyes.

Except for their birth dates (within a year of mine), acquired from hints when I added Dotty and Robert to my family tree, I had no idea what they looked like. I observed older couples and families with children reserve seats at the long picnic tables. They did this with place settings pulled out of their bags—plates, glasses, and utensils. At that point, I noticed paper plates and plastic utensils were missing from the food tables. I certainly hadn't thought to bring my own. Before I had time to worry, a man came toward me, saying, "Are you Peggy?" He introduced himself as Robert and ushered me over to Dotty, who was organizing place settings for the three of us.

I had already put my cheesecake sampler on the plastic-covered tables along with the other potluck contributions. Sturdy handmade signs—Main Course, Vegetarian, Sides, Desserts, and so forth—created a self-organizing method in place of the usual chaos of food receivers and arrangers. There was an abundance of food.

Around one o'clock we were asked to take our places, and Pastor Ron said grace. In my family, we are lucky if someone says grace over our Thanksgiving and Christmas dinners, let alone at reunion potlucks. The prayer was perfect for the pavilion filled with relatives, many of whom didn't seem to know each other, beside a pretty church in the mountains.

I was introduced to another reunion innovation, which prevented a stampede or long lines. First, those eighty years and above were invited to the food tables. Families with children under ten went next. The rest of us joined in as the lines diminished. Lines, because with the food spread over many tables with space between, people did not wait long to fill their plates.

While we ate, a big yellow bucket was passed around to collect money. This was done casually, without pressure to contribute. Everyone had brought everything, even their own plates and cups, some paper, some dishes that would be taken home to be washed.

So, what is the money for? I wondered, but didn't ask.

None of the reunions I'd ever attended collected money. When most had finished eating, Robyn stood up and called the meeting to order. She wasn't just an organizer, but the president for this year's event. I had never heard of a reunion having a president! She systematically went through the agenda using Robert's Rules of Order. The minutes and treasurer's report from last year's reunion were read and formally accepted. The committees and various people responsible for tasks were thanked. Pastor Ron was handed a donation for the church kitchen and gift cards appeared. Aha! The mystery of the money bucket solved.

Categories fitting the event were called out: family with the most generations present, couple whose combined ages was the highest, youngest baby, oldest woman and oldest man in attendance. For traveling the longest distance, I was awarded a $20 Walmart gift card. The meeting ended after a new slate of officers was voted in for 2018.

With her duties as president over, Robyn took me into the church and unrolled an enormous family tree that showed her extended family and their ancestors. Spread over two long rectangular tables, the multicolored chart with boxes, circles, and lines was surprisingly easy to follow.

Robyn showed me the records from previous reunions. I paged through the signatures of those who had attended over the years. Perhaps, years from now, someone looking through the book will see my name under the year 2017.

I was curious about the history of the church. Jonathan Gordner had paid $25 for the land for the purpose of building a church and creating a cemetery. The original church, built in 1890, was destroyed by fire in 1970 and a few years later rebuilt and renamed St. John.

The area seemed to ooze with history. I wished I could have accepted Heather's invitation to see the old Temple-Gordner farm just down the road. Heather and I had begun exchanging emails when I found her aunt Mary and I were a DNA match. Heather had come from Connecticut. If not for me, she probably would have won the "farthest" traveler prize.

Sarah Lore & George Gordner
Great-great-grandparents
Gardner Cemetery Unityville, PA

From one month to the next, my feelings changed and even my memory of them. Also changeable was how I justified, even to myself, what I was interested in or why I did something. Preserving emails seemed the best way to document my experiences.

Date: June 28, 1917

Subject: Reunion all set

Heather,

I made my travel plans and am really looking forward to it--though not even sure why, because family is who you grew up with and, at my age, my friends are like my extended family. But there really is something special about thinking of being around people who I got my genes from. Don't "they" say now that much of who we are and how we behave derives from how we are born--our genes!

Peggy

I said my goodbyes to my paternal grandmother's relatives. It was time to meet relatives of Grandfather Ward Ikeler. There didn't seem to be a local Ikeler reunion, but I had tracked down and

spoken with two of James' first cousins: Donna and Helen Jean.

Both encouraged me to visit. Luckily, they lived near each other in Columbia County, just south of where the reunion was held. To avoid more mountain driving I hoped to meet both in the same home, but neither could make the trip to the other's house. Donna's eyesight was failing and Helen Jean had given up driving.

It had been fun meeting distant cousins at the big reunion, especially those I had been in communication with, but Donna and Helen Jean were different. They were James' first cousins. I would have known them like I knew some of my parents' first cousins. My grandfather was Uncle Ward to them and they had known my great-grandparents. Of course, all my own great-grandparents were dead by the time I was born, so it seemed foolish to think that meant something.

And even more foolish because of James' estrangement from the family—these cousins hadn't even known he existed when they were growing up. I found that out a month before my trip when I first contacted Donna. At the time, I was using Skype for long-distance calls and worried that no one would answer without a name and phone number on caller ID. We older people who grew up with heavy, black, dial phones are used to being surprised by who's on the other end of the line.

A woman answered right away, but since the person from whom I had gotten the number wasn't sure Donna was still alive, the first moments of the call were confusing to both of us: "This is Peggy Nicholson. Is this Donna?" Her answer was clear, but she sounded disoriented:

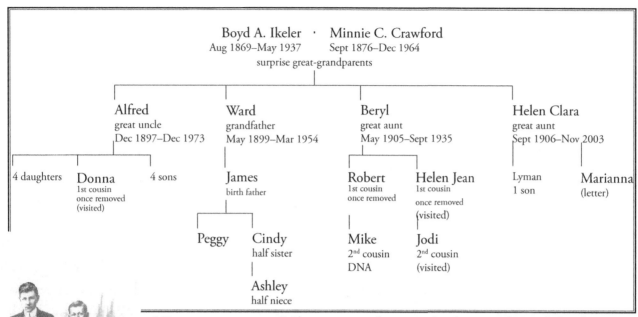

Boyd A. Ikeler · Minnie C. Crawford
Aug 1869–May 1937   Sept 1876–Dec 1964
surprise great-grandparents

Alfred
great uncle
Dec 1897–Dec 1973

Ward
grandfather
May 1899–Mar 1954

Beryl
great aunt
May 1905–Sept 1935

Helen Clara
great aunt
Sept 1906–Nov 2003

4 daughters

Donna
1st cousin
once removed
(visited)

4 sons

James
birth father

Robert
1st cousin
once removed

Helen Jean
1st cousin
once removed
(visited)

Lyman
1 son

Marianna
(letter)

Peggy

Cindy
half sister

Mike
2nd cousin
DNA

Jodi
2nd cousin
(visited)

Ashley
half niece

**Minnie & Boyd Ikeler
L>R Helen Clara,
Alfred, Ward, Beryl**

"Give me a minute." She was repeating my name, as though trying to remember who I was.

I reassured her that she didn't know me and to end her confusion got right to the point: "I'm calling about your brother Ward's son, your cousin James." With the mention that I was James' daughter, she said, "Oh, wait, I have to sit down. I've had strokes."

Once she got her bearings, Donna spoke almost nonstop for the next twenty minutes. When she finished, I had the answer to a puzzle and knew why I ended up on a wild goose chase looking for a grandfather named Laubach. Donna's married name was Laubach!

As an adult, Donna first heard about James from an older sister: "One day, Zoe said, 'I wonder whatever happened to Jimmy?' I said, 'Who's Jimmy?' I didn't even know Uncle Ward had a child!'"

Donna was already an experienced genealogist and had no trouble locating James' family in Florida. By that time, James had passed away. Thinking someone in the family would be interested, she

sent a letter with photographs and family names to James' son. When the letter and its contents got passed to Cindy, somehow Donna's surname got mixed up with the other names and that is how Laubach got into Ashely's tree,

What a relief! I could finally close the door on the mystery of the Laubach-Ikeler name confusion. I don't consider all the extra time searching a lost cause. I identified many cousins along the way and learned about building family trees and combing through records. I was relieved that I never asked a Laubach descendant to submit to a DNA test.

When I hung up, I realized Donna had not asked about my mother. Perhaps she assumed I was the child of one of James' wives. We spoke a couple times more, but the subject of motherhood never came up. She mostly liked talking to me about others who were researching the Ikelers and discussing the arrangements for our upcoming meeting,

I knew Donna was eager to see me, but planning the shortest route between the big reunion, these "one-on-one" reunions, and the return to Harrisburg meant Helen Jean, the other cousin, got to meet me first. Helen Jean lived with her daughter, Jodi, in the countryside in a one-story house with a huge yard. A creek ran the length of the property. The three of us sat on the large porch and drank lemonade.

**Peggy & Helen Jean
Jersey Shore**

July 30, 2017

**Peggy & Donna
Bloomsburg**

My previous interaction with Helen Jean was also by phone. Donna had suggested I call her and had given me her number. Helen Jean, too, picked up my unidentifiable Skype call. Having been forewarned by Donna about my story, she launched into her own, "Yes, Beryl was my mother and she died when I was only twenty-eight days old." I was impressed with her unabashed openness as she told me about living first with her aunt, then her grandmother, and later passed around among other relatives. "I never knew where I was going to be. My dad would come by and say, 'You're going to stay with so and so.' I felt like no one wanted me." Helen Jean talked about feeling she "wasn't worth anything." She credited her husband with helping her realize she was lovable. "It took me a long time to believe *I was somebody*."

Because of the phone conversation we had shared weeks earlier, when I arrived at Helen Jean's home, I felt like I was dropping in on a long-time relative. She brought out a photograph album and pointed out various relatives. Both her daughter (my second cousin) and I were entertained by seeing our great-grandparents, aunts and uncles, and hearing funny bits of history. After her daughter went inside, Helen Jean and I talked about the books each was writing. Hers was about her upbringing, a

result of her mother's early death, and how she overcame a negative self-image. I suggested the title, "I Am Worth Something."

Mine was about the experience of finding, in late age, an unsuspected biological father. My emotional adjustment was different too. The feelings catching up with me were, "This is what I'm like," and "There never was anything wrong with me."

I was enjoying myself, but having scheduled approximately an hour for each cousin, I swallowed my last gulp of lemonade, and we said our goodbyes with hugs.

Thirty minutes later I was in the center of Bloomsburg, parked on the street across from the row house where Donna lived with her husband. The narrow rooms were filled with furniture, photographs, and mementos. After talking for a while in the living room, we went to the second floor to look at large framed photographs of the Ikeler family farm and relatives.

She gave me a copy of a photo which, along with other relatives, showed James as a tiny baby held by his grandmother, with his father standing behind their chair. I'm glad to have the photo, but it is symbolic. James is barely visible among the blankets. I was right. Looking at Grandfather Ward without memories to bring him alive, my reaction was exactly like Noah's: "So what."

In contrast, when Donna handed me a copy of an eighteen-page handwritten letter, I was overcome by her trust in me. The letter, filled with personal memories, was written by another of the Ikeler first cousins, to his much younger half sister. In addition to the family history the content provided, the letter gave me a link to Ward's third sibling, Helen Clara. The warmth conveyed in the first paragraph and the date make these first cousins once removed seem not that far away.

Dear Marianna,

I have been giving some serious thought regarding a gift for a little sister who is about to be married. What does an older brother, some 34 years older, have to give or share—maybe some memories. These memories have been mine alone for a long time, unfortunately some of them have tarnished, some are dim, some are as bright as the day I rec'd them, even brighter because they have been rolling around in this greying head of mine.

11/28/1914 Your brother, Lyman

Donna held our goodbye hug long. She had been disappointed not to hear from James' family after sending the letter and photos. She was happy when I assured her they had arrived, and that the names in the letter had helped me identify the

Ikelers, if in a roundabout way. Donna said, "You've given me peace of mind."

Driving back to Harrisburg, relaxed and satisfied having met many members of my surprise family, I thought about the past months of both distressing and delightful discoveries. Searching for "new" relatives brought me to "old" relatives, the ones I grew up with. And I learned that on my mother's and biological father's sides, I was the many-times-great-grandchild of immigrants who had come from Germany and built the churches, schools, and cemeteries of central Pennsylvania.

35

From Relatives to Family to Friends

BACK in Harrisburg, Susan greeted me as I came in the door. Before she had time to reach for the bottle so I could join her in a glass of wine, I fell into her arms, sobbing. Between the tears, I was mumbling about—

… my daddy and his family and the new families which weren't really mine—but they could have been. These strangers I met weren't the people I grew up with, the people I knew all my life and felt close to, but they might as well have been. James' brother, Uncle Donald, was similar to my dad's brother, Uncle Bob. Any photo taken at the Gordner-Stackhouse reunion could have been swapped with one from a Nicholson gathering. I was feeling pulled between my real family and my genetic family.

Then the burst of tears and jumbled flow of words dissolved because I didn't have to choose—both families were mine. I was back to my cheerful, present-time self. I ran upstairs and changed into sitting-around clothes, before flopping into one of the overstuffed recliners in the living room. Susan, already settled into hers, muted the TV.

After I went over highlights of the reunion in Unityville and the visit to my Ikeler cousins in Columbia County, our conversation meandered for hours—interrupted only by trips to the kitchen to refill our glasses. While talking about what we had been through together over the past seven months, I noticed how much my emotions had seesawed: from suspense, to surprise, then suspicion, back to sadness, and finally to serenity.

We enjoyed gossiping about others' reactions. There was a lot to turn over in our minds. Much could not be proven, but I was firm about what I thought was true.

Some people think my parents had to know I wasn't "their" child. I don't know why. There is proof she had an "encounter" close to the time of my conception with both Daddy and James. Even if she suspected, which I'm sure she didn't, she'd have no way of finding out. Back then, blood tests could eliminate a father in some cases, but not prove paternity.

I told Susan, "I'm lucky! I haven't lost anything, though there were times when I felt I had. And I've gained a set of new relatives. Some have even begun to feel like family."

We talked until we couldn't keep our eyes open and had to go to bed.

Amazing and wonderful are words to describe the impact these months have meant to Susan and me. We always knew we were relatives though forty years passed without us setting eyes on each other. Then we reconnected and slipped into being family—attending family events together. Not every family member becomes a friend, but Susan and I seemed to be moving in that direction.

If not for a conflict in timing, which was initially upsetting to me, I wouldn't have been with Susan and Angie. When Susan heard the friend I normally stay with would be out of town, she sent a long email inviting me to their home. Promises about my comfort for sleeping, eating, and freedom to come and go were included.

Before my stayover, though I can't point to anything in particular, Susan seemed a bit formal and distant to me. I couldn't imagine being comfortable as a houseguest nor did I believe she would be relaxed having me. We did enjoy our regular, long phone conversations, which began after I received my surprise DNA results. The phone, because I could not be cajoled into Facebook messaging, and text messages were blocked from my flip phone.

Sharing a home with Susan and Angie created a special sort of intimacy. There is no better way to get to know people, even longtime relatives, than shuffling around in the morning in PJs, drinking coffee, and watching chatty, entertaining TV news. We had plenty of time at night to learn more about each other's lives.

Peggy & Susan Harrisburg October 2017

One evening, as Susan told me the "story of her life," I could have fallen off my chair. I was amazed to learn how wrong my perception was about her. I knew she had been a middle-school teacher for the Harrisburg school system for forty years. That seemed to go along with what I imagined: a modest, proper, routine-oriented, conventional woman who went to college right after high school, got a job, and settled down.

I couldn't have been more wrong. Susan, graduating from high school in 1965, found herself in the middle of the sixties cultural revolution. She married a childhood friend during her sophomore year of college (birth control pills were for married women). A year later she "ran away" and eventually ended up moving out west. Leaving out the juicy details of boyfriends and marriages, she moved back to Pennsylvania and created a commune on her grandparents' old, run-down farm.

Eventually finishing her degree, Susan began her career as a teacher, where she met Angie. They fell in love and have been together for twenty years. The comfortable, roomy house where they live now is in an older, beautiful community, perfect for walking their big labs, Buster and Daisy.

During my next visit, I will ask if knowing me better has altered how she thinks of me.

Since the trip to meet my surprise relatives in July 2017, I've been back to Harrisburg two or three times. I haven't deserted my good friend, and if she is in town I do spend some nights with her. For the remainder of the time, I settle in with Susan and Angie. The nightly ritual we established on my first visit is set in stone: wine in front of the TV, solving the problems of education and the world, and laughing along with the pretend-news comedy shows.

Doris, Susan, Angie with Marg at her 80th Birthday Party March 2000

After Mom and Aunt Doris died, Susan and I would have likely lost touch again. My venture into DNA testing and genealogy created an opportunity for Susan and me to come to know each other. We knew we were relatives—though we had no contact, Then we reunited as family—seeing each other once in a while. Finally we became friends—a consistent and loving relationship. People say you can choose your friends, not your family. Susan and I have the best of both worlds. I love when she says I am the sister she never had. I've begun to think of myself as having five sisters!

36

Who Belongs in My Family Tree?

I adore my online tree filled with the names of relatives I know and love, distant cousins I never expect to meet, and long-dead fifth- and sixth-great-grandparents. It is much easier and more fun to work on than the spreadsheet I began and abandoned years ago. Once Susan motivated me to register for an account and explained the idea of shared trees, I was hooked. My tree is shared with many relatives, and I can view twenty-five trees others have shared with me. Most of us are second to fourth and even fifth cousins. If we choose, we can allow each other to see "living" people.

I'm generous about which relatives belong in my tree. Others may have to think it through. Including a step-parent is an individual choice and may depend upon a child's age when a parent remarries or the nature of the relationship. Genealogical trees don't always coincide with biological relationships and combining the two makes sense. Susan, seven years old when her widowed mother remarried, includes both her father's and her step-father's families in her tree.

Upon hearing my story, someone referred to Frank Nicholson as my step-father. I blew up inside, but calmly explained, "We don't share DNA, but he is as much my legal father as if I had been born to him." It's irrelevant given that he is dead, but my relationship to him in the eyes of the law is the same as that of my sisters. His name is on my birth certificate, and he and my mother were not only married when I was born, but when I was conceived as well. I don't know if the last event means anything in my case.

Polyclinic Hospital
Mr. and Mrs. Frank Nicholson, Jr., 620 Kelker street, a daughter, Margaret Ann Nicholson, August 28. Mrs. Nicholson was Miss Margaret Martin.

Once I knew Cindy and I shared DNA, I moved James from the separate tree I had started for him into my tree and began

Michael (b. 1962) with mom Peggy, grandfather Pop-pop (Nick), held by great-grandmother (Mamie Nicholson)

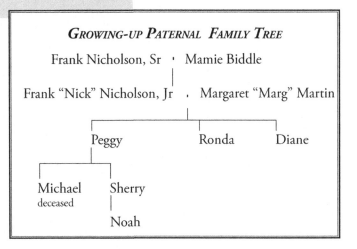

Growing-up Paternal Family Tree

Frank Nicholson, Sr ⋅ Mamie Biddle

Frank "Nick" Nicholson, Jr ⋅ Margaret "Marg" Martin

Peggy   Ronda   Diane

Michael   Sherry
deceased

Noah

**Boyd & Minnie Ikeler, grandparents of James (in blanket)
standing: Helen Clara, Elberta, Ward, Alfred/Fannie, Beryl**

adding as many ancestors and descendants of his that I could find.

From the moment I heard that my biological father "didn't practice safe sex!" my curiosity was aroused. If a new person shows up in the close family category and Cindy is among our shared matches, I'd be almost certain the person was a child of James. An exchange of messages would reveal if he or she were in a situation similar to mine, with a surprise birth father. If there is another sibling, I do hope he or she is a "he."

Although we had male cousins to play with, my sisters and I felt the one thing missing in our home was a brother. As we, and especially my mother, grew older, it became obvious we weren't getting one. A brother, though "half," would still be fun to have, even at my age. I wouldn't hesitate to include in my tree anyone genetically connected to James.

What hadn't occurred until recently was that my Nicholson sisters could also come across a half sibling. Nick was a young, single man when access to birth control was limited. During World War II, Daddy was away from home for months at a time. A good-looking young man in uniform probably would have had the opportunity for a liaison. A woman in Philadelphia or Oregon may have assumed, like Mom, that her pregnancy was the result of relations with her husband.

Thinking about Daddy having another child led me to, "Oh, I understand how Kim must have felt hearing about me." Her reaction was different from Cindy's. Kim did not seem as eager to

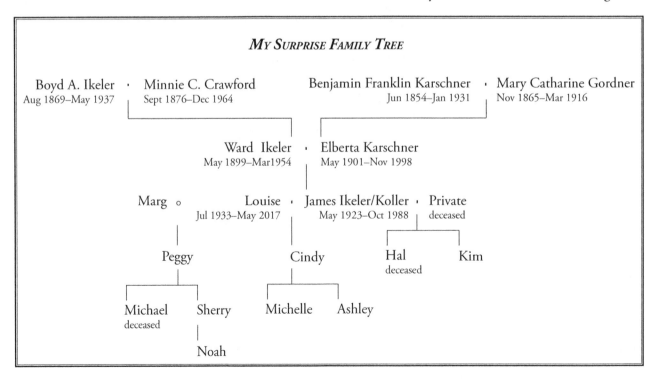

My Surprise Family Tree

Boyd A. Ikeler · Minnie C. Crawford   Benjamin Franklin Karschner · Mary Catharine Gordner
Aug 1869–May 1937   Sept 1876–Dec 1964   Jun 1854–Jan 1931   Nov 1865–Mar 1916

Ward Ikeler · Elberta Karschner
May 1899–Mar1954   May 1901–Nov 1998

Marg ○   Louise · James Ikeler/Koller · Private
Jul 1933–May 2017   May 1923–Oct 1988   deceased

Peggy   Cindy   Hal   Kim
deceased

Michael   Sherry   Michelle   Ashley
deceased

Noah

communicate with me. I called her once. Maybe it was an inconvenient time and place, but she didn't suggest I phone later, nor did she call back. But then, Kim's relationship to James was different from Cindy's. She grew up with her father.

Thinking of my own resistance to the idea of a strange woman acting as if she has some attachment to my daddy places Kim's initial reaction in another light. But does that make sense? Nick isn't my biological father. But Nick—I hate calling him that—was as much a father to me as James was to Kim. I feel entitled to my resentment to that possible half sibling out there in DNA-land. That person, if there is one, won't be going into my tree.

Best of all, I didn't have to give up my "real" daddy, but I did have to add a biological father to my family tree. Daddy, my grandma and grandpa, and the cousins I grew up with are in my tree. They are there to stay.

37

Searching for Ancestors, Hoping for Descendants

My attention had been focused on two streams of research: tracing my genetic match from Ashley to my new paternal family's ancestors and their descendants, and filling in my tree on the Martin and Nicholson lineages. Then all of a sudden, I realized my son Michael could have produced a child.

Always told in the spirit of joking around was the story of a little boy born to a friend of Michael's. I wasn't living nearby at the time, but family members said he looked like Michael. I suppose if it had been true, the mother would have at least asked for financial support. But perhaps this child, or another, was conceived under circumstances similar to my own—one in which the mother assumed another man, not Michael, was the baby's father.

What if there were a child, really an adult by now, and we met? Would he or she remind me of my son? Just as I inquired about my biological father, I would be asked, "What was Michael like?" Imposing height was his most noticeable physical feature—six feet six inches tall, but not big or heavy. He never achieved that middle-aged look, even by forty-nine. Trimmed light-brownish hair and an easy smile. Everyone who met

Michael liked him. He wasn't a mean or judgmental person. And he was creative and very intelligent.

Every morning, first thing, I turn on the computer and look for a new name near the very top of my matches. I pretend my interest is in matches who will lead me to old ancestors. Deep down I hope for a surprise—a descendant fathered by Michael.

**Michael & Max
Purcellville, VA
Thanksgiving 2002**

38

Like *Birth* Father, Like Daughter?

PVT. JAMES B. KOLLER

3-Times Wounded Soldier Is Home

Three times wounded and recipient of several meritorious awards resulting from action in the invasion of France, Pvt. James B. Koller, Harrisburg paratrooper, has just returned home.

Private Koller, who entered France on D-Day, wears the Purple Heart and the Bronze Star, and holds the Presidential Citation, the British Citation and the French Government Citation.

A former employe of the Harrisburg Steel Corporation, Private Koller entered the Army on December 7, 1942. He is the son of Mr. and Mrs. Elwood Koller, 1716 North Fifth street. His wife is the former Miss Talitha Jane Lerch, daughter of Mr. and Mrs. Harry Lerch, 2028 North Sixth street.

The private is on a 22-day furlough following which he will report to the Asheville, N. C., redistribution center.

My biological father was a paratrooper during World War II and jumped out of an airplane on D-Day in Normandy. James was wounded and evacuated to a hospital in England. After recovering, he was sent back to France. He was furloughed back to the US with a Purple Heart, Bronze Star, and Presidential, French, and British Citations. Official documentation of James' participation in D-Day and an account of his injury was easy to find online. Harrisburg newspapers reported on James' return home after suffering two additional injuries.

His interest in travel and his bravery during war are my favorite things about him. My desire to travel began at nine years old when I believed digging a hole in my backyard would get me to China. When I finally did begin traveling on my own in my thirties, friends looked askance when I told them about my adventures:

- In Dubrovnik, I told a boyfriend to keep an eye on the couple from the balcony, while I ran down to interrupt the man's unwelcome advances to the woman he was with.

- At a party in Berlin, the first person I spoke with told me I had just crashed a top-government reception with high-level security.

- I walked with a man down

a long dirt road into the forest. On my way to a small mountain town in Morocco, I had accepted his invitation to have lunch at his sister's home.

Someone will invariably ask, "Weren't you afraid?"

My answer has always been, "No, I wasn't afraid." Now I will add, "It's not in my *genes* to be afraid."

Of course, in contrast to James, I had a choice of where I was and never put myself in what I perceived as a dangerous situation.

People who know me and my family might argue, "You aren't like that because of your genes. You had a mother who never seemed afraid and who trusted everyone. Your personality is more from growing up around her." This is undeniable. The chaotic environment I grew up in must have affected my behavior as well as my mind—it was either face fear directly or hide under the

Peggy walks past guard onto grounds of school in China.
Teacher spots her wandering the halls.
Drags Peggy into classroom to give English lesson.
Teacher takes her on scooter through terrifying traffic to lunch.
July 2007

covers and shake. I guess my mother also deserves credit for what others consider the adventuresome and brave part of me: on the one hand, from the way she herself unabashedly faced the world, and on the other, by unintentional adverse effects.

There were other, not as admirable, aspects of James' personality. Did I also share these? Over our second beer, the evening I had dinner with Cindy, I asked, "What did James do for a living?"

"He was in collections, and by the time he moved to Florida he was pretty well off and had his own company."

Though I had a vague idea about what debt collectors do, I researched collection agencies. The qualities needed to be successful included what I had heard about James' personality: If you're a sensitive person and don't like confrontation, the job isn't for you. You need to be calm but can't be a doormat either. People will come up with thousands of excuses as to why they haven't paid, and you need to be assertive to ensure payments are made.

This characterization fit perfectly with traits Cindy's mother Louise shared with me about James. I was prepared to be wary of what she, as an ex-wife, might tell me, but I didn't need to worry. During our phone conversation, she was willing to share less than flattering characteristics of James' business and family behaviors. But she described observable behaviors rather than subjective personal adjectives. Louise also made it clear she wouldn't want to say more because he was Cindy's father.

When I asked about their courtship, Louise described his pursuit of her as aggressive. About his work, she used the word *obstinate*, or I got that impression from what she said. Evidently, he was willing to say anything to obtain the information he needed to track people down. "He would make up stuff to find out where people lived."

Well, if your job is to collect debts, you must find the people who owe them, don't you?

I don't have to make up stuff to get people to tell me almost anything. But then, I'm not after their money, just the things they would have preferred to keep secret. I don't hesitate to ask for what I want. Some people say, "Peggy's aggressive and obstinate and not willing to give up easily."

James was not likely to be afraid of confrontation. All my life I have struggled with people's reactions, only recently recognizing how terrifying a loud, argumentative conversation can be to some—even though I thought we were merely discussing an idea or clarifying a misunderstanding.

James and my daddy didn't seem to have much in common, except they both died before their sixty-sixth birthdays—James seven months, Daddy one. They lived those years very differently. I don't know what prompted James' first marriage, but his brother told me she was the prettiest girl in Harrisburg. The marriage didn't last long. After his second wife Louise divorced him, James did not maintain consistent contact with their daughter Cindy. When he passed away James was still married to his third wife, twenty years his junior, with whom he had had two more children. As an adult, Cindy eventually reconciled with her dad.

I was able to grow up in a stable home with two sisters, an ever-present mother, and an intermittent male presence because Daddy worked the 3–11 shift during the week and all day Saturday at a part-time job. But he remained married to Mom and was a father figure in our home.

Some men take longer to mature and settle down. I have the impression impulsiveness played a role in James' life. My own dad wasn't perfect. I remember Mom telling me that in the early years of their marriage, "Your daddy would miss work sometimes because he was out drinking with his friends." My sisters and I only remember them going out together in the evenings.

My own story mimics James' life more than Daddy's. I married twice, divorcing both times and allowed my children to grow up with their father. I remained involved in their lives and saw them often.

I find comfort in knowing about my birth father's negative personality traits because they seem familiar. I have them too. He had his good points, certainly courage and resilience, but he doesn't sound like a consistently nice or reliable person. Good friends, people who know me well, say I am generous and caring. But acquaintances may not have the same opinion.

A counselor asked if being aggressive and knowing what you want could be positively perceived as perseverance. And if *obstinacy* could be interpreted as *persistence*—accomplishing projects. After thinking it over, the phrases about James and me rang in my head for a while.

I like telling people, "There never was anything wrong with me. I'm smart, strong, and successful, just like my surprise father."

39

What If There Had Been No Ashley?

SOMETIMES the question creeps into my mind, "What would have happened if Ashley hadn't tested her DNA or had chosen a different company?" Ashley was hoping to prove her paternal grandmother was Native American. A company other than Ancestry.com would have been a better choice for that purpose. What if Ashley had known that?

And, "What if I had gotten tested years before Ashley?" I dismissed a suggestion by a friend to compare my sisters' DNA to mine long before public databases were available. If her opinion that I had a different father was correct, I would have had no way of finding out who he was. I had no interest in wanting to learn who my father *wasn't*. Easily available matching services were introduced around 2012. Ashley submitted a test kit in early 2016. It's not an exaggeration to say I would have been living in suspenseful agony for years. Curiosity is one of my blessed and cursed personality traits—it would have driven me crazy.

Ashley was there for me! When I put myself in the position of others, I become anxious and squirmy. Now I understand better what some people who were adopted feel. I'm in contact with two DNA matches who have been searching for biological parents for years. There must be a difference between *not knowing* who a biological parent is all your life than, as happened to me, *knowing*, and then all of a sudden (because of DNA results) *not knowing*.

A tinge of discomfort arises when I think how it felt the moment I saw Ashley's mysterious match and the weeks that followed until the results for Ronda, Diane, and Cindy ended all doubt. There were times I was heartbroken and felt alone, as if I didn't have a paternal side to my family tree. Once I *knew* for sure who belonged in that biological paternal spot in my tree, I could face all that came with the discovery.

I met James' daughter, Cindy. Later, I even had the opportunity to speak by phone with her mother, James' second wife. I met Donald, James' brother, who was open and accepting. They generously shared their experiences with me, and this made all the difference in the world. I could never meet James, but at least he was not a complete unknown, like a black hole out there somewhere in the universe.

James Koller
~1985

40

Nothing Has Changed, Everything Is Different

Not everyone faced with a surprise father reacts as I did. One writer described the shame he felt upon learning the man whose genealogical history he had spent years developing was not his biological father. He kept the news mostly to himself until he wrote a book. I felt no shame, and from the beginning told anyone who would listen, "I did my DNA and the daddy who raised me might not be my biological father." Once there was no doubt, I changed the "might not be" to "was not." For me there's an element of pride in the experience, but I admit this makes no sense. Of course, in contrast to the writer, I hadn't invested years in researching my paternal ancestors, nor did I spend summer holidays visiting old family homesteads.

From the first phone call with Uncle Donald, I felt as close and warm toward him as if I had always known he was my relative. It was similar to what happened with Susan after we reconnected. Those two share the same biological and genealog-

Introducing Sherry & Noah to Uncle Donald & Barb January 2018

ical kinship with me, one on each side of my family: Donald is my father's half brother. Susan is my mother's half sister.

I had the opportunity to visit with each of my sisters in Harrisburg after discovering we weren't full sisters. Ronda flew from Hawaii for a family visit in the fall. Diane drove up from Philadelphia in the winter when Sherry, Noah, and I flew to Harrisburg for the Pennsylvania Farm Show. I was hoping against hope Noah could see a real snowstorm, but there were only flurries.

My sisters and I didn't spend more than a few hours together, and other relatives were always present. Someone watching would have seen nothing out of the ordinary. Everyone hugged and chatted away as always. Though I can verbalize, "They are my *half* sisters," the words have no meaning. Ronda is my sister. Diane is my sister. I asked each if her feelings toward me had changed. I can't repeat the exact words because my sisters were rather vague in their responses. Something to the effect: "Of course not, why even ask. I'm not into psychoanalyzing everything, like you do." I was pleased by the first part of the answer and shrugged off the second, as the putdown it was meant to be.

As for Cindy and Kim, I do think of them as *half* sisters. Without shared experiences that generate conversations, such as "Remember the trip to Atlantic City …" or "Remember at Daddy's funeral …," there is a void. That said, Cindy and I have already shared over a year of phone conversations and a dinner. I'm sure to meet more family. I'm eager to get to know Kim. I can't wait to meet Ashley. She has no idea how important she is to me.

After many years of blaming others—primarily my mother—for bad habits that made my life difficult, now I'm my own worst enemy. This isn't to say a less chaotic home life wouldn't have been preferable: one that provided the piano lessons I begged for, support to attend the university that accepted me, and resolving conflicts rather than screaming and hitting.

On the other hand, my mother always seemed more modern to me than my friends' mothers. She was independent, creative, and had a sense of humor. I admired her for not bowing to the traditional norms of a neat and orderly house over her children's needs.

Long before it became fashionable, Mom adopted the attitude of today's parents—indulgence over discipline—but without one snippet of "helicoptering." Relatives dropping by might find cracker crumbs on the floor made by three little girls roller-skating through the house. Her attitude was: "It's raining out. They have to have somewhere to play."

It seems to me that Marg Martin Nicholson was in the vanguard of women who, not as part of a movement, but individually assumed equality with men. (Though, in many ways, this was not legally possible before the 1970s.) If, besides controlling the finances, making major family decisions, and working outside the home, this included sexual equality, more power to her. This view of her is consistent with her other unique characteristics, like her ability to beat most men at pool.

Over the months of my DNA and ancestry pursuit, with each new discovery, friends and strangers would ask, "How do you feel?" My answers changed over time, depending upon the moment I was asked. Now that all is said and done, I say, "I feel exhilarated."

This feeling of exhilaration isn't visible from the outside. It is how I feel inside, how I feel about myself. If I had known earlier about my biological father's characteristics, would I have felt something was wrong with me? What if I had lived with him? Does anyone know how *she* would feel growing up in an alternate family?

The words "This is who I am." kept going through my head. I accept myself, but not in the sense of accepting my bad characteristics, which I never had a problem doing. This new "This is who I am." is about finally accepting my good qualities, which set me apart. (Without ever having understood why.)

Perhaps my mother's encounter was a special gift to me. After all, where would I be if it hadn't happened? Born with one man's genes and raised by another, I'm grateful for having learned about James and especially for finding my surprise family who opened their lives and hearts to me.

Margaret Briner Martin Nicholson
Linglestown American Legion
December 31, 2002

Epilogue

IN March 2003, Jae Fisher and I were alone in the car, driving from my mother's memorial service to the graveside. We were old friends from when I lived in Philadelphia, and she had driven more than two hours to Harrisburg to attend the service. After spending more than twenty-five years sharing stories about ourselves and our families, we knew a lot about each other's lives. Jae had been observing my two sisters and me as we greeted family and old friends of our parents.

Mom had been in the foreground of Daddy's funeral in 1986, while we sisters played more or less an equal role. With our mother's death, my feeling of responsibility and my take-charge manner were in full force. Jae's tone was decisive when she stated, "I think you have a different father."

I countered, "Oh, come on, we don't look that much different and our coloring is the same." I'm the oldest, tallest, and smaller-breasted sister, and look more like my mother. Ronda's the shortest, and is big-boned with wavy hair like our dad's. Diane, the youngest, is between us in height and weight, and takes after our paternal aunts in build.

"It's not your physical differences, it's your personality and intellect," Jae explained. "The difference in your behavior, your way of thinking." She just couldn't believe I came from the same father.

Jae knew my sisters and had heard more from me about them, mostly worries and complaints. I loved them both, but she was right about Ronda and Diane and our differences. Growing up and for a long while, before I had a chance to live away from my family, there were times I thought something was wrong with me. "There has to be some genetic basis for the variation," she said.

"What difference would it make now," I stated. Jae responded as if I had asked a question: "You can stop feeling guilty."

I thought she was nuts about a different father—the idea was too weird. My parents conceived me during the first year of their marriage—the honeymoon period. Perhaps there was cheating later, but that early?

A few weeks after Mom's funeral service, I was visiting eighty-year-old Aunt Doris, my mother's sister. I brought up the subject: "My friend thinks I have a different father." My aunt immediately replied, "I know who it is," and went on talking, "Marg was in love with Shakes." I knew who she was talking about. William Shakespeare was a classmate of Mom's. I grew up hearing about him and other school friends of my parents. Aunt Doris, younger by three years, had lots of stories about what kind of person my mom was, using words like "flirt" and "loose." Supposedly, Mom went to Atlantic City with someone—was it Shakes?—without wearing her wedding ring and while pregnant with my sister Ronda.

Aunt Doris went on at length about Marg and her plentiful dates and then started on other stories, especially those that showed her older sister's meanness. I can't count the times I heard the one about the day they were coming home from school, which Aunt Doris repeated word for word every time she told the story:

I guess I wasn't walking fast enough to keep up. Marg got mad and threw her own good fur hat off the Maclay Street bridge. When we got home, she started crying, blaming me for what she did! And, of course, Mother would always take up for Marg. I was the ugly, red-haired girl. Your mother could never do anything wrong in the eyes of Mother and Dad!

Doris & Marg

From my own experience, I knew my mother could be mean at times and would blame others for her own mistakes. She never admitted to being wrong—about anything—even if caught in the act. Aunt Doris came by her jealousy honestly because her red hair and freckles couldn't compete with Marg's black, lustrous hair, blue eyes, and clear skin. I actually heard Nana, my grandmother, say what an ugly baby Doris was.

Aunt Doris eventually circled back to the birth-father proposition. "When your mom and dad were dating and they had a fight, Marg would use it as an excuse to go out with Shakes."

After rambling on for a while, Aunt Doris stopped short, seeming to realize she was straying into a world of make-believe. She knew Marg was self-indulgent and a flirt, but she couldn't believe her sister would recklessly get pregnant by someone other than her husband. She ended with a firm, "No, I'm sure Nick is your daddy."

Aunt Doris' statement reassured me, but it was her reaction when I brought the subject up that convinced me I didn't have a different father. When she ended her speculations, neither was she taking back her compromising stories about my mother, nor was she hiding a sixty-year-old secret. If there

were a secret to keep, and my mother and Aunt Doris managed to hide it all those years, she would have reacted differently. Determined to take the information to her grave, her response might have been, "Oh, that's not true. Your friend is wrong." Or, if she thought I had the right to know, "Yes, that's true. Now that both your mom and dad are gone, I can tell you."

Instead, Aunt Doris had been open and spontaneous with her gossipy stories about her older sister. The stories about Mom and her flirtations were not new to me. I had heard them from Aunt Doris over the years. But Jae's speculations and Aunt Doris' "I know who it is!" created a dramatic story and once in a while added fun to family conversations. For the ten years that followed, I didn't give the "You have a different father" idea much thought unless someone or something brought it to my attention.

One such time was when Jae was visiting for a long weekend. We found ourselves stuck in the house because St. Augustine was in the midst of one of its fall storms of strong winds and heavy rain. Jae and I stayed in our PJs all day, sat on the couch with snacks, and watched daytime TV shows.

Our favorite was *The Maury Show*. DNA test results determining paternity were announced on air to men who looked delighted, dazed, or devastated by Maury's dramatic, "You *are*—or—You are *not* the father of …!"

Going to a private laboratory to compare my DNA to my sisters', while not impossible, would have been expensive. Jae and I talked, more so joked, about getting free DNA testing with Maury. I decided to send an email asking *The Maury Show* to test my adult sisters and me, suggesting this would provide an interesting variation from the usual format of determining the paternity of young children. A return email thanked me for my interest.

Subject: Be A Guest

Date: Friday, March 22, 2013

Thank you for your interest in being a guest on The Maury Show! Due to the overwhelming response, we appreciate your patience on getting back to you! Know that we read every email but if you do not hear from us in a timely manner please call (888) 456-2879.

Again, thank you and we look forward to seeing you at The Maury Show!

I never did call. But Jae and I promised each other that someday we would be raucous members of Maury's audience.

Yes, Jae put the thought in my head at my mother's memorial service, but I knew, as did Aunt Doris, that the daddy who raised me *was* my father. Fourteen years later, DNA results proved otherwise. Thinking back through the years from my earliest memory forward, nothing was said and no behavior was shown from either parent to suggest otherwise.

Anyone who knew my parents would agree

Peggy & Mom
Rotterdam 1994

with me about their authenticity and openness. Those who missed the pleasure will have to take my word for it. They loved and fought, showing sweet affection one day and saying nasty things the next. While my sisters and I were growing up, we never saw any indication that either parent had a relationship outside the marriage. Mom seemed incapable of keeping secrets, and Daddy would not

have kept such a suspicion to himself. Sometimes I was awakened from a deep sleep by one of their horrible fights and run into their bedroom, begging them to stop. With me in sight, I am sure if either doubted my paternity, the opportunity to pierce the other with a revelation or an accusation would have been too much to resist.

Do I think my mother knew and kept it to herself? Knowing how many of her thoughts and how much of her day-to-day life she shared with her mother, her sister, and me—anyone who would listen—I can't imagine. She had no boundaries. After gaining an education, I was catapulted from working in factories and restaurants to professional positions. One of the hardest things I had to learn was how to behave appropriately and not say everything that came into my head. As one colleague pointed out, not meaning it as a compliment, "Where are your defenses?"

Did my mother bury it deep inside? It is possible to keep disturbing thoughts hidden from consciousness. Many therapeutic models can be found that deal with the effect of the unconscious on behavior. It was easy for me to imagine she had consciously erased the encounter, because I had my own experience with doing so. For ten years I believed I "had to get married" because of an accidental pregnancy. Eventually I was able to acknowledge that I chose to become pregnant.

During the years after Daddy died, it seems logical that my mother might have said something if she had suspicions. But without a DNA test, there could be no answer. My appearance didn't hold the key. My looks were not distinctive from my Nicholson cousins, I fit right in. In meeting Cindy and Donald, neither reacted to my looks.

My eyes are blue, and before turning gray my hair was dark brown. Daddy had dark hair and blue eyes. James too.

Margaret (Peggy) Nicholson
April 2018

Acknowledgements

My Surprise Family: Find Your Ancestry Story would not have been completed without the practical help and emotional support of many people. My first mention of gratitude goes to the people, strangers at first, who graciously responded to my message requests for information. To them, as well as to all the relatives I grew up with, I owe a big thank you for allowing me to use "real" names.

Those reading this book will know how indebted I am to Susan Martin. She was by my side every step of the way. Her comments on the first draft were invaluable. From start to finish, Susan's responses gave me the courage to keep going. She had always been a relative and, like some members of my surprise family, now is part of my life.

Christy Sheffield Sanford's extensive assistance and editing were indispensable. She pushed me to reach deeper and put what I found into words. Christy creatively used the photograph of me with my parents for the perfect book cover.

Susan Ciccantelli contributed hours, reading yet another revision in my quest to make a convoluted story easier to follow. By phone, she listened and quelled my fears about publishing my story. Susan says love for the project was her motivation.

Rebecca Richardson, at Heritage Designs LLC, did a beautiful job with the design and formatting of the book. Without her, the book would consist primarily of words with a few photos and inscrutable diagrams. Rebecca's equanimity under pressure was the perfect match for my erratic methods.

Jae Fisher was so pleased with an early draft, I doubted her objectivity. She reassured me that the informality: "I felt like you were talking to me" was better than my usual formal, academic tone.

Members of the Catalonia Critique group improved the quality of my prose. Their complaints moved most, if not all, "technical stuff" to the end: Roger Carlson, Christy Sheffield Sanford, Susie Schecter, and Judith White.

Early readers whose feedback helped me determine the range and depth of content were: Christina Frazier whose background in biology was an asset. Ruth Hope whose edits clarified my approach to the story. Monika Ward and Murrell Weissinger whose honest criticism made all the difference.

In the manuscript stage, readers graciously served as copyeditors: Linda Warren, Peg Miceli, Antoinette Wallace, Jennie Spratt, and Judy Fegen. In addition to reading the story, Julie Gatlin tested the *Find Your Ancestry Story* manual. Judy Parr proofed the instructions. Special mention goes to Richard Hebert for catching all that was missed. Only I'm responsible for any lingering errors.

Sasan Rahmatian, who never read a word until he bought the published book, was there when I needed help, as always. He returned my frantic calls and used the means-ends hierarchy to get me back on track.

My gratitude to the members of my surprise family is unbounded and can be read throughout the book. Barbara and Donald Koller deserve a special thank you. Their acceptance was critical in converting what began as a disappointing event into a positive and joyful experience.

FIND YOUR ANCESTRY STORY

Contents

Organization of Book

Companies with sophisticated technology are allowing—even encouraging—us to test our DNA. My story is about taking part in this DNA adventure only to find a mystery genetic match. I was confronted with the challenge of searching for an unknown person on a futuristic Website, while building a family tree around my parents and ancestors dragged me into the past. *My Surprise Family* tells that story. Included are explanations of how I identified DNA matches and developed my family tree.

Find Your Ancestry Story refers both to the "how to" anecdotes (in gray boxes) interspersed throughout Parts I-V and to Sections One through Four that follow.

Much more help is available on Ancestry.com's Website, at many third-party online sites, and from hard copy manuals. Some people find these forms of instruction overwhelming and won't attempt their use. This book is for them, many of whom are my dear friends and relatives.

I focus primarily on Ancestry.com, the company I used. (I suggest you research companies before making a choice.) Comments and instructions are based on my understanding of how the Website works.

Though I present this material as introductory, early readers who considered themselves well informed with Ancestry.com's Website found new ideas in these pages.

HELP: Support Center

The Ancestry.com Support Center provides easily accessible, clearly written instructions with up-to-date screenshots. My "click here, click there" instructions, accurate upon publication, will become out-of-date as the Website changes.

For any topic you look up, the Support Center will have related links with interesting information that may catch your eye.

1. On logging in, Ancestry.com opens to a screen with a Black Bar Menu across the top: HOME, TREES, SEARCH, DNA, HELP, EXTRAS

2. Choose HELP

3. From the drop-down menu, click on SUPPORT CENTER

4. The next screen opens to a Support Home page with the words: What can we help you with?

5. Immediately below those words is a box into which you can type a few words.

In contrast to what your teacher told you, complete sentences are unnecessary. Use the name of a feature you need help with such as "shared matches," "share DNA," or describe your problem using ordinary words.

When you aren't looking for a specific feature you may want to look farther down the page at the various links under the main headings: AncestryDNA – Ancestry Account - Featured Articles

When using the Support Center, I usually open a second window on my computer to look back and forth between the instructions and my account.

NOTES

Organization of Find Your Ancestry Story

Registering with Ancestry.com for a guest account and ordering a DNA kit was straightforward. I knew to ignore the screens that seemed to imply a Subscription was required to get started with my family tree and sending in my DNA kit. But after beginning my tree, I was confused by which Website features were available with the guest account, which would be included in the cost of obtaining my DNA Results, and exactly how I would benefit from a paid Subscription.

There are genealogists who have had Subscriptions for years and eventually submit DNA kits. This was Susan's experience, and it was not surprising she could not distinguish between the features accessible because she now had DNA Results and which had been available with the Subscription.

My three-step process with Ancestry.com allowed me to see these differences clearly. For weeks I had a free guest account (Section One) while waiting for my DNA Results. Then I had a month or so of viewing and experimenting with my DNA Results without a Subscription (Section Two). Once I paid for my Subscription, I was able to enjoy the combined features (Section Four). Though I never had a Subscription without DNA Results, it is not difficult to imagine its usefulness for genealogical research (Section Three).

By organizing the material in this format, I hope to make it easier to understand what features are available under which conditions: free, one-time cost, and an ongoing cost. Showing what can be accomplished with the Website by Section helps to see how the features interact with each other. These were the distinctions as I understood them at the time this book was published.

Ancestry.com is bound to change screen design, symbols, and add new features. For this reason, I rarely include screenshots. The ultimate value of these sections lies not in the exact "click here-click there" steps, but in knowing there is a feature available. My intention is to increase your comfort in using the Website and prepare you to use the Support Center, where you will find up-to-the-minute screenshots and instructions.

What is a Feature?

I use the term "feature" to refer to a function which serves one or more purposes. For example, Shared Matches is a feature that allows you to create a list of people who share DNA with two (or more) other matches. This feature is useful in identifying to which family lineage a person belongs.

Caution: I focused on the features I used and that were helpful to me. I am proficient with Ancestry.com's Website, but the company does make periodic changes. Any policy, procedure, or instructions mentioned in this book may have changed by the time of publication. I have already discarded "click here-click there" instructions for two features, because a Website redesign eliminated the need to search by making certain pieces of information visible.

NOTES

Section One:
Guest Account — Creating & Sharing Trees

There is no cost for a guest account, nor for creating and sharing (sending and receiving) family trees. Compare the tree-building features that are without cost in this section to the tree-viewing and research features described in Section Four which requires a paid Subscription.

Don't be confused, when, after building a tree, Ancestry.com begins sending "Tree Hints" letting you know records are available. In the beginning, you will see indexed records and perhaps handwritten originals. You might even be able to save a record or two to a person in your tree. Eventually, you will be directed instead to a screen with Subscription offers. But if you are content with the features in this section, you can carry on indefinitely with a guest account.

Register For A Guest Account

1. Go to Ancestry.com.
2. Click GET STARTED.
3. On the next screen, click GET STARTED. You will see various options for a cost which you can ignore.
4. On the next screen, fill in the form: First, Last Name, Email, and Password.

These details can be changed anytime via your Account settings. Remember to record the email and password.

Sharing a Family Tree: Accept an Invitation

Perhaps you have no interest in participating in DNA testing or creating an online family tree, but there are relatives who want to share trees with you. After registering for a free Ancestry.com account, accepting an invitation to view someone else's tree

is as easy as clicking on a link in an email. You can begin the process without an account, but the least confusing method is to register first. Be sure to give the same email you used to register the account to the person inviting you to view a tree. These directions assume you do have a registered account. After accepting an invitation, you may want to read about the different ways to view trees.

Accept an Invitation to View a Family Tree

1. You will receive a message from Ancestry.com in your email announcing you have been invited to view a tree. (If you don't receive the email soon after you know someone has sent it, check your spam folder or have the sender check the spelling of your email. I've had both mistakes happen more than once.)
2. Click on Explore Now INSIDE the email.
3. The tree appears on the screen, and the name of the tree will have been placed in your TREES menu.

To find the tree again:

1. On logging in, Ancestry.com opens to a screen with a Black Bar Menu across the top: HOME, TREES, SEARCH, DNA, HELP, EXTRAS
2. Click on TREES.
3. Click on the name of the family tree you want to view.

Create A Family Tree

The directions for creating a family tree assume you have a registered account.

1. On logging in, Ancestry.com opens to a screen with a Black Bar Menu across the

top: HOME, TREES, SEARCH, DNA, HELP, EXTRAS

2. Choose TREES: Start a New Tree (If you already have a tree, but want to begin another, click on Create and Manage Trees).

3. The next page will have a Pedigree form with +Add Yourself in the left most box.

4. Click +Add Yourself to open the "add a person form."

5. Add your first and last name, check mark the correct gender and status: living.

6. Add your birth date and location. Remember to click SAVE when entering or changing this form.

7. Add either your mother or father. When you click SAVE for this second person, a screen appears with a box to personalize the name of your tree. Allow the default setting to remain checked for public tree.

8. The next page shows your two-person tree in Pedigree view.

9. Read Family Tree Views next or skip down to Building your Family Tree.

Family Tree Views

Family, Pedigree, List of All People, and Profile are different ways of viewing family trees and each serves a different purpose. Invited guests can navigate to all the viewing options, but cannot change anything in the tree. Owners and those invited as editors can use the different views to add and adjust people and relationships.

1. Family View

The traditional, vertical Family View shows each

Navigation Suggestion

There are many ways to navigate within your account. My advice is to always begin from the Black Bar Menu which is across the top of your screen after logging in. The main tabs are: HOME, TREES, SEARCH, DNA, HELP, EXTRAS

The tabs will take you to drop-down menus which will vary depending upon whether you have created a family tree, tested your DNA, or paid for a Subscription.

Links other than the Black Bar Menu often lead to screens for ordering kits, buying a Subscription, or upgrading a Subscription.

person, along with his or her name and birth-death years, in a blue or pink box (unless replaced with a photo) with connecting lines to parents, siblings, and children. This view graphically shows family units. Because of space limitations, not all family units can be seen at the same time. For example, when a woman's family is visible, a link in the form of two tiny boxes is attached to her husband's box to indicate his family is hidden. Clicking the link will show his family and hide hers.

2. Pedigree View

The horizontal or Pedigree view shows only direct ancestors: parents, grandparents, great-grandparents, and so forth. In other words, your family pedigree begins with you, goes to your parents, then to their parents, and so forth.

In both Family or Pedigree Views, tapping on an individual will enlarge his or her box to show the dates and locations, if filled in, of the person's birth and death. There are tabs for other tasks as well: Profile, Search, Quick edit, and a symbol for Tools.

3. List of All People View

List of All People is a three-column view of all the people in a tree. The headings are Name, Birth (date and place), and Death (date and place). I use this view to check for duplicates, locating people not attached to the main tree, and finding unusually spelled or misspelled names.

Near the top of the page are search boxes. You can search by letter of the alphabet, first name, and/or last name. Use letters for names that have numerous spellings. I have distant family members who spell their name Kockendorfer, while others use Kockenderfer.

There are Gordners and Gardners—I was told one brother got fed up with mixed-up mail delivery and changed the o to an a. First or last name is useful when you are not sure if someone is using a maiden or married name for a woman.

My favorite way to use this view is to compare my family tree to another's in search of mutual ancestors. When I come across a long list of Garmans in a match's tree, I open a second window, go to List of All People in my tree, type in Garman, and compare side by side. At any time, clicking on a name in either tree will take you into the Profile View for that person. (This works for those who have DNA results and a Subscription.)

4. Profile View

In Profile View, a page is dedicated to one person. The person's name is at the top of the page. If family members have been added, these are listed down the right side of the page: parents, siblings, spouse(s), and children. Click the Profile tab on a person's name box for this view. (This is different from a DNA Profile page.)

To switch back from Profile view, click the tiny tree symbol beside the name of the tree or use the TOOLS menu in the top, right-hand corner: View in Tree. Other navigation symbols can be seen along the left side of the page in Family or Pedigree Views. These can be used to switch views, find home person, and change the size of the name boxes.

Building your Family Tree

Once you have a tree started, you can continue adding people—your other parent, go "backwards" for grandparents, or "forward" with children and grandchildren. Stay in the Pedigree View or click the symbol for Family Tree View, which is the view Susan uses to add people. I prefer to add people from a person's tree Profile View.

Adding People – Switching to Profile View

1. Click the person's name box for tab menu:

Profile – Search – Quick Edit – Symbols for Tools.

2. Choose Profile – screen opens with person's name across the top of the page, boxes for family down the right-hand side of page.

3. Adding relatives can be done three ways:

   • Click on mother, father, spouse tab

   • From "Add" drop-down menu, top right

   • From "Add Family," at end of list

4. After completing the form, don't forget to SAVE.

When adding a child to a parent in the Pedigree and Family Tree Views, be sure the default setting on the bottom of the form indicates the correct parents. Depending on the size of your monitor and the number of family groups in your tree, you may have trouble seeing generation levels or all siblings in a family. But in the Profile View, you can see a person's immediate family all listed in one place: his or her parents, spouses, and children. A "Sibling" link is below the parents. I feel like I have more control using the Profile View when adding to or editing my tree.

Gallery: Uploading Personal Items

Photographs and documents in your possession can be uploaded and attached to a person from Profile View. Click on Gallery for the "upload media" link.

You and those with whom you share trees will be able to view these items, but a Subscription is required to view Gallery items in public trees.

Edit: Edit Relationships

The Edit Relationships feature is useful for fixing relationship mistakes and reconnecting people to the main tree. You can also link or unlink people to see how kinships are affected. (See Tangled Branches & Kinship Diagram) I found that developing a correct tree without making mistakes was impossible. This feature allows you to disconnect relationships without deleting people—you will even get a reassuring pop-up reminder. For example, you may assign a son the wrong mother but not want to delete either because they both belong in your tree. You can disconnect the "wrong" mother without deleting her, and on the same screen, connect the correct mother (or add a new one if need be).

Don't forget to deal with the disconnected mother if she has become a "floater." A floater is a person in your tree who, on purpose or by accident, is not attached to anyone else in the tree. The Ancestry.com Support Center refers to floaters as "unrelated people."

You may not know you have a floater until you find yourself thinking as I did one day: "I am sure I added Edward Garman, where is he?" Floaters can be found in two ways:

1. If you know the name of someone, but don't see him where you expected (as the son or father of someone), use Find Person.

2. If you aren't sure of the exact spelling, use List of All People to search by letter.

Everyone in your tree, connected or not, is in List of All People. If you find the person, click on his or her name and go to Profile View. Is there a kinship term designating your relationship to the person? If not, the person is either not connected to anyone else in the tree or is connected to others, but none of them are connected to the main tree. Use the Edit Relationship feature to re-connect the person or group to the main tree. (See Skipping Generations & Adding Unrelated People)

Skipping Generations & Adding Unrelated People

When adding people to a tree, you can neither skip generations (to have a grandparent, there must be a parent), nor can you add a sibling to someone unless they share a parent. If you don't know the name of the missing person, use any word (unknown, Mother, Father) or a symbol such as a question mark as a first or last name.

This is an important feature. Without it, many of us would have people technically in our trees (they can be seen in Find a Person or List of All People) but not connected to anyone else in the tree. Unless you are an experienced user, it is best to avoid these unrelated people (Ancestry.com's term). Floaters (my term) can accidentally be created when you are using Edit Relationships.

There are reasons to have a person or a family group temporarily not connected to others in your tree. Perhaps there is a genealogical roadblock or a DNA connection you're working on. Once you have resolved the issue, use the Edit Relationships to reconnect a person or group of people to the main tree.

Tools: Merge with Duplicate

You may notice you have two of what appears to be the same person in your tree. Go to the Profile View of one, and use Tools: Merge with Duplicate to compare the two. Information for both (birth and death dates, parents, etc.) will be shown. Click cancel if they are different people or, if they are the same, after choosing which facts are correct, click merge.

After adding a confusing group of siblings, their spouses, and children, I use List of All People to compare people by surnames to ensure I haven't created duplicates. If I have, I use the merge feature to correct my mistake.

Share Family Trees: Send an Invitation

Once you have created a family tree, you may want to invite others to view the tree. Convenience is one of the main reasons to share trees among those who are working on the same family but maintaining separate trees. Links to shared trees are found in the TREES drop-down menu.

1. Open the tree you want to share by clicking on the name of the tree in the TREES menu.

2. After the tree is open, click on the name of

the tree, in the upper left corner.

3. From the drop-down menu, choose Sharing.

4. Invite People: Click on Email.

5. On the next screen, type in the person's email (Use the email they have registered on Ancestry.com.)

6. Add a personal message, if desired. I include the following message, unless I'm inviting an experienced person: "To view my family tree, first login to your Ancestry.com account. Then come back to this email and click on the invitation. My tree will appear on the screen. From then on, the tree can be found by name under your TREES menu."

Create & Manage Tree Invitations

Both the trees you create and the trees you are invited to view are listed under the Black Bar Menu: TREES. If a tree seems to have disappeared, don't worry. The drop-down menu shows only so many. At the bottom of the list click on Create & Manage Trees. You will find two links: "My Trees" and "Trees Shared with Me." From here, you can manage your tree invitations.

When you invite someone to view your family tree, there are two options that can be changed. These options are preset to the most secure level. This means you don't have to worry that you will accidentally share more information or allow greater access than you intended.

To alter "Role" and "Living Information" for each person you've invited to view your tree:

1. On logging in, Ancestry.com opens to a screen with a Black Bar Menu across the top: HOME, TREES, SEARCH, DNA, HELP, EXTRAS

2. Choose TREES.

3. From the drop-down menu, click on Create and Manage Trees.

4. The next screen opens to My Trees with the name(s) of the tree(s) you created. Before moving to Step 5, notice that there is also a link for Trees Shared with Me. You can't change settings for trees shared with you, but it's good to know where you can see the entire list of trees shared with you.

5. On the My Trees screen, columns are titled Name, Date Modified, Role, and Tools. In the Role column, Owner (meaning you) is listed for each tree. Just below that, click on "person" or "people invited." ("Invite family" means no one has been invited or has accepted an invitation.)

6. The next screen lists the individuals with whom you shared a tree. There is a Role and Living Person setting for each person.

Role

The Role feature changes a person's status and can define whether they are a Guest, Contributor, or Editor. Click on the small "i" for the activities an individual will have permission to do if you change the role from guest. Use the drop-down menu to change the role. Before doing so, be sure you understand Editor allows the person to do everything you can do except delete the tree.

"Living" Information

By putting a check mark next to "Can See Living People" you allow the person you've shared the tree with to see the names (and other information) of those still alive. Without this checked, the security of those still living is maintained.

Notes

Section Two:
One-Time Cost For DNA Results

Anyone can buy any number of DNA Kits to use or give away. Once a kit is purchased there is no additional cost for activating the kit, the laboratory analysis, and other features related to the DNA results:

- DNA Matches
- Link DNA to your family tree
- Amount of DNA (centiMorgans) shared with each match
- Messaging system to communicate with matches
- Share DNA with others
- Migrations (previously Genetic Communities)
- Ethnicity Estimate

Referring to features above as free is not technically correct. If you think of having paid for them with the cost of the kit, it will help you understand why the features that combine DNA Results with public trees (e.g., Shared Ancestor Hints and DNA Circles) do have a cost. Viewing public trees requires a paid Subscription (Section Four).

For each feature below, I begin the navigation instructions beginning with the login step.

Your DNA Match Summary

Ancestry.com sends an email letting you know your DNA Results have been posted to your account. If you are working on your tree, as I was, you may find your DNA Results have arrived before you see the email announcement. Every half hour, I took a break from my tree and clicked on the DNA tab. All of a sudden, there was "Your DNA Results Summary" in my menu. I clicked with eager anticipation. If you jump ahead by clicking

VIEW ALL DNA MATCHES to scroll through your DNA Matches as I did, come back later to read this overview.

Find "Your DNA Results Summary"

1. On logging in, Ancestry.com opens to a screen with a Black Bar Menu across the top: HOME, TREES, SEARCH, DNA, HELP, EXTRAS

2. Choose DNA.

3. From the drop-down menu, click on Your DNA Results Summary (You can go directly to DNA Matches, but you would miss seeing if new ones have been added unless you have more than 1000.)

4. The screen that appears has three good-sized boxes, left to right:

DNA Story – Ethnicity Estimate & Migrations

The Website is continually adjusting these two items. For more information see the most recent AncestryDNA White Paper Ethnicity Estimate 2018. Additional comments can be found in and near chapter 20. Finding Migrations is the last item in this section.

DNA Matches

There are four links in the DNA Matches box.

1. Shared Ancestor Hints – Collects into one list any match who has the same common ancestor in his or her tree as you have in yours. (Section Four).

2. Starred Matches – Collects into one list individual matches you have marked with a star. (I mark special matches to find them quickly. You may have other reasons to use this feature.)

3. 4th cousins and closer – This is the number of DNA close matches, but links to all DNA matches. The number will increase to 1000. Once you have 1001 matches, the number will show as 1000+. (I watched my 1000 for about a week before it turned to 1000+.)

4. VIEW ALL DNA MATCHES – This is a link to all your DNA matches.

DNA Circles – (Section Four)

DNA Matches & Categories

DNA Matches are listed *hierarchically* by the amount of DNA shared with you. The word hierarchy ought to help you remember that the people/matches are ranked from the highest shared amount to the lowest. No matter which sort feature you use—kinship categories, shared, starred, new, search by family surname / location—those in the list will always be ranked hierarchically by amount of DNA from the top to the bottom of the page.

Matches are grouped into categories, but you only see those for which you have DNA matches. The cousin heading is used loosely and includes grandparents, grandchildren, aunts, and uncles. The divisions between each cousin level are based on approximate calculations of expected ranges and averages for the amount of shared DNA for a kindship level.

- Parent/Child
- Immediate Relative
- Close Family
- 1st Cousin
- 2nd Cousin
- 3rd Cousin
- 4th Cousin
- Distant Cousin

Link DNA to a Family Tree

Linking your DNA to a family tree is free, and I encourage you to do so. When people take this step, it is easier to figure out relationships. There are two features that use these DNA-linked trees to identify relatives automatically: Shared Ancestor Hints and DNA Circles. Because viewing public family trees is involved, a Subscription is needed to benefit from these features, which are described in Section Four.

1. On logging in, Ancestry.com opens to a screen with a Black Bar Menu across the top: HOME, TREES, SEARCH, DNA, HELP, EXTRAS

2. Click on DNA.

3. From the drop-down menu, choose Your DNA Results Summary.

4. On the next screen, below Hello, "*your name*" is a sentence: This test is shown to matches as "*your name:*" Link to Tree.

5. (Your name will be there if you have already linked your DNA.)

6. Click Link to Tree.

7. From the drop-down menu, choose a tree (or start a new tree). From there you will be led through either process.

8. Be sure to refresh the screen—click something else, then return to Your DNA Results Summary. The Link to Tree tab will now be replaced with Linked to "*your name.*"

9. To edit your choice, begin with Your DNA Results Summary screen. Click on the Settings tab (little gear) in the top right corner. The next screen is the Test settings for "*your name*" screen.

Shared DNA / CentiMorgans (cMs)

How closely two people are related is indicated by the amount of shared DNA which is measured in centiMorgans (cMs). All things being equal (which often are not), the higher the amount of shared cMs, the closer the relationship. The highest amounts identify parent/child and full siblings. From there the uncertainty begins, and as the amount decreases, the more difficult it becomes to

What's a CentiMorgan?

For our purpose in identifying genetic matches, think of a centiMorgan as a piece of DNA and the number of centiMorgans shared as the amount of DNA shared. Otherwise, we are confronted with language such as the following: A centiMorgan is a unit for measuring genetic linkage. It is defined as the distance between chromosome positions (also termed loci or markers) for which the expected average number of intervening chromosomal crossovers in a single generation is 0.01. It is often used to infer distance along a chromosome. However, it is not a true physical distance.

determine the nature of the relationship. For example, is the matching relative who shares ~400 cMs a first cousin once removed, a half first cousin, or a great-great-aunt?

A person's DNA is comprised of 50 percent from each parent, but this doesn't mean that each sibling gets the same 50 percent. Nor does the DNA inherited from each parent have an equal amount from each grandparent. More importantly, for each sibling or cousin, the specific "pieces" of DNA received from parents, grandparents, great-grandparents, and so on differs. Because of this, one of four siblings may not share DNA with a third cousin who matches the other three. (See Tossed Salad, Not Pureed Soup)

Except for parent/child and siblings, the amount of shared DNA which identifies kinship levels can vary quite a lot. Someone listed in the 2nd cousin category could instead be your first cousin or perhaps your third. Early on I found a second cousin listed under the 3rd cousin category.

Understanding Shared DNA

The Website was recently changed, and you no longer have to search to see the amount of cMs you share with a match. The amount is shown immediately below a match's screen name after the words Shared DNA. There is more information about what this number means specific to the match you are viewing.

Click the display name of the person. The next screen has two options:

1. Click on (What does this mean?) after "Possible range" to see various relationships you might have with your match.

2. Click the small "i" after "Confidence." The number of centiMorgans is repeated. (This was the previous method for finding the amount.) Then click on What does this mean?

A box opens with the heading: What does the match confidence score mean?

A chart shows the likelihood, represented by a percent, that the shared genes were inherited (identical by descent—IBD). The alternative is that the shared genes happened by chance (identical by state—IBS). You will notice the percent is converted into words referred to as a Confidence Score. These are the terms—extremely high, high, good, and moderate—you see next to the screen names of your matches.

For example, if you share 45-60 cMs with someone, the likelihood is 99 percent certain that you have a common ancestor with that person. You will see Confidence: Very High next to his or her name. When you share 30-45 cMs there is a 95 percent chance you are related to a common ancestor. Matches who share this amount of DNA are listed under 4th cousins with the label Confidence: Good. The problem with such a chart is that we tend to forget that the range of DNA shared among 4th cousins can actually range from 0 to 107!

At the bottom of the box is a link to Ancestry.com's White Paper on DNA Matching. I find these scientific reports written for non-scientific readers fascinating.

DNA results will not determine "how" you are related to someone, only that you are related. You may be familiar with the person and already know the relationship. I knew Susan was my aunt, not my cousin. Susan knew Beth was her daughter, not her mother. Relatives unfamiliar with each other can quickly find their relationship if both have well-developed family trees.

In the case of surprise DNA findings, such as unknown biological relationships and adoptions, ages are a helpful predictor. There is no confusion between who is parent, who is child or who is grandparent, who is grandchild. It's more confusing among cousins and aunt/niece, especially when age doesn't follow expected generational levels. Susan's age (similar to mine) puts her in my generation, but for DNA and kinship associations, she's in my mother's generation.

Shared Matches (Triangulation)

Identifying where a DNA match belongs in our family tree depends upon finding the relative from whom we've inherited our shared DNA—our most recent common ancestor, abbreviated as MRCA. The MRCA is the answer to the question: How are we related?

The Shared Matches feature reveals which of your matches share DNA with you and another match. This is sometimes referred to as triangulation. As you scroll through the list of matches you may recognize relatives who sent in DNA. Depending upon who has been tested, you may be able to determine on which line of your family tree an unknown DNA match belongs.

To understand how the feature works, first consider an ideal but unrealistic condition: Your mother, father, and you have been tested. You are looking at an unknown DNA match and click the shared matches tab. If your mother's name is included in the shared matches, the unknown match belongs to your mother's family. If your father's name is there, the match is on your father's side. Imagine the same process if all four of your grandparents had been tested.

I'm mostly interacting with older people whose parents are not alive or younger people who are seeking unknown birth parents. With the increasing popularity and lower costs of testing among younger people, perhaps this scenario—of four grandparents having been tested—may not be so unrealistic.

The problem with this simplistic description is that DNA is "unevenly" inherited. In other words, DNA is unevenly distributed among relatives. This creates a situation in which the range for the expected amount of shared DNA at a kinship level is quite wide. For example, the expected average for third cousins is 74 cMs, but one pair could share zero and another pair of cousins share 217. For this reason, the answer to a relationship question is not always clear.

The more relatives who have been tested, the easier the process. When identification of matches is going to be difficult because of adoption or an unknown parent or grandparent, understanding how Shared Matches operates is more important because you can "drill down" to isolate those matches who seem to have the same grandparents or great-grandparents.

How to Find Shared Matches

1. On logging in, Ancestry.com opens to a screen with a Black Bar Menu across the top: HOME, TREES, SEARCH, DNA, HELP, EXTRAS

2. Choose DNA.

3. From the drop-down menu, click on DNA Matches.

4. The next screen shows the people with whom you share DNA.

5. Click the display name of a person whose shared matches you want to see.

6. The next screen brings up the person alone on the page, along with three tabs:

   • Pedigree and Surnames

   • Shared Matches

- Map and Locations

7. Click on the Shared Matches tab.

8. The next page shows matches who share DNA with you and the person selected.

Shared Matches are listed hierarchically by the amount of DNA shared with you, NOT with the other person. I mistakenly thought the list was reordered to show how close these matches were with the person selected. For more information about how this affects your searches, see Sharing DNA Results.

If the amount of shared DNA is below a certain threshold, those relatives will not be included as a shared match. This could cause you to misinterpret relationships. Sharing DNA Results among relatives is one way to overcome this problem.

Add Note

For the first few days, I didn't notice the "add note" link just under the names of matches when viewing them. I record names of Shared Matches and our common ancestor (if I have figured it out). If I'm still puzzling over a match, I record familiar surnames from a family tree.

Add Note

1. Click the View Match tab of a DNA Match.

2. Click on Add Note.

3. Type in any information you choose.

4. Click on SAVE before leaving the page.

5. To add to or edit the note, return to this location and click on the pencil symbol to open the text box.

When scrolling through your DNA matches and viewing shared matches, you can click on the note symbol to see information you recorded instead of having to leave the page to go to Profile View.

Accessing the Note

1. A link to the Note appears next to the person's name.

2. Clicking the Note symbol allows you to view the information.

Sorting DNA Matches

Once you are familiar with the main hierarchical list of DNA matches, as they appear in the categories, you may want to sort them in other ways. These choices are listed at the top of the page on the left above the first person.

Each of the three sort features mentioned below can be viewed by either:

RELATIONSHIP – Your matches are listed by the amount of DNA. This is the default setting.

DATE – Your matches are listed by most recently tested.

Sort by:

1. (Shared Ancestor) HINT– These are matches who have the same common ancestor in your respective trees. (Do not confuse the Hint with Tree Hints—a suggested record for a person in your tree.)

2. NEW – These are matches you haven't viewed by clicking on their display names or View Match. The blue dot beside a name changes color when you have viewed someone, but if you want to make someone "new" again, you can do so by clicking on the dot to restore the blue color.

3. STARRED – Individual matches you have chosen to mark with a star. (I mark special matches to find them quickly. You may have other reasons to use this feature.)

Messaging with DNA Matches

Ancestry.com provides an email-type system for interaction with others in the DNA database. You won't have any trouble finding the Send Message tab when you View a Match or the Contact "*screen name*" tab when in Ancestry Profile. The main problem is noticing that you have received a message. Look for the tiny envelope symbol to the far right in the Black Bar Menu. If you have received messages, a minuscule number on the envelope indicates how many are waiting to be read.

I have gotten responses from DNA matches more than a year after sending a message. The person usually apologizes, saying they didn't notice. Ancestry.com would do well to make the message indicator more visible.

I include my phone number and email address in all my messages. I like to think the more open and willing I am to share, the more people respond. Not everyone would be as comfortable doing this. My early messages only asked others for information, now I provide details before asking my questions. Be friendly to all your relatives or anyone asking for help, no matter how distant the relationship.

Sharing / Linking DNA Results

The words "sharing" and "sending" may give the impression that when you share DNA with someone, you are *giving* them your DNA results. But sharing DNA only provides a link so that someone can view your matches from his/her own account. When you share DNA, the best part is that you can now each see how much DNA the other person shares with his or her matches.

There are different sharing options. A collaborator can add information to a "note," while the owner maintains control for downloading, sharing with others, or deleting the DNA.

When small amounts of DNA are involved, a match usually won't appear in Shared Matches (triangulation). This can be confusing, and you can be misled about family lines. I have a match on my mother's paternal line, but don't know if it is through my great-grandmother or great-grandfather. Cousins from each of those lineages shared DNA with me which made identification of other matches much easier. Amounts as small as 10 cMs are sufficient to put me on the right track.

1. On logging in, Ancestry.com opens to a screen with a Black Bar Menu across the top: HOME, TREES, SEARCH, DNA, HELP, EXTRAS

2. Choose Your DNA Results Summary.

3. On the next page, click on the SETTINGS tab on the top right of the page.

4. Next page, bottom left, under DNA Result Access, click on Add a Person.

5. A small window opens—type in the email address the person uses with their Ancestry.com account.

Leave the role as view, or if the person is going to help you, choose collaborator. Do not choose manager, unless you are sure you understand the authority you are turning over to the other person.

In cases of adoption or surprise DNA results, sharing DNA can speed the process.

Migrations

Ethnicity Estimates only correlate your DNA to others and use those others to produce probabilities that your ancient ancestors may have come from the same geographic area.

Migrations are different because they, like the DNA Circles, are based on shared DNA. The Migrations feature is about your genes and your recent ancestors. According to the AncestryDNA White Paper, "Migrations show broader patterns in a large network likely to represent recent shared history. The result is that we can identify clusters of living individuals that share large amounts of DNA due to specific, recent shared history."

You will find informative historical overviews, and people from your tree will be identified with geographic areas.

1. On logging in, Ancestry.com opens to a screen with a Black Bar Menu across the top: HOME, TREES, SEARCH, DNA, HELP, EXTRAS

2. Choose DNA.

3. From the drop-down menu, click on DNA Story.

4. Migrations are on the right side of the page, immediately under Ethnicity Estimates. (The term will appear only if a Migration group has been associated with your DNA.)

NOTES

SECTION THREE:
Subscription (without DNA Results)

A paid Subscription provides access to public trees, unlocks the archives of record collections (e.g., census records, death/birth certificates, etc.), and allows you to attach these documents to people in your family tree.

Upon stopping your Subscription, you won't be able to see Ancestry.com attached records (images you upload are not affected). However, the records remain appropriately attached, and if you re-subscribe they will be visible.

Many people choose never to participate in DNA testing and are content with access to genealogical records and public family trees. In other words, the price you pay for a Subscription is the same with or without DNA testing.

An Ancestry.com Subscription works similarly to a magazine Subscription. There is typically a discount price for first-time subscribers which increases to the standard rate upon renewal. The Subscription price increases if you choose more databases. Rates vary depending upon monthly, semi-annual, or annual payments.

I was amazed at how much there was to learn from the documents, photographs, and stories available online about my relatives. There was so much to absorb about what day-to-day life was like in the US not many years before we, who are alive today, were born. Imagine how strange it would be on today's census form to see questions asking if someone can read and write, has a radio, and not just the number of children born to a woman, but the number still alive?

Combining a Subscription with DNA results, as I did, allowed me to more easily identify DNA Matches by viewing their public trees. Also, any Shared Ancestor Hints and DNA Circles were viewable.

Marriage & Death Certificates

Much of what is available through a Subscription—viewing trees and searching / attaching records—has been discussed in the memoir parts of this book. I wanted to point out how valuable access to marriage and death certificates are. This is because the names of the parents, as well as the mother's birth name, are included. If you are lucky, as I was, it did not take long to find the names of many of my fourth-great-grandparents!

Advanced Searching

In my efforts to develop my genealogical past I've been using Tree Hints and help from others. New to both DNA matching and genealogy, the readily available materials have been more than enough for much of what I've wanted to accomplish. But there are some issues that will require more advanced forms of research. Susan and I are stuck at Irvin Martin's grandfather Simon. We haven't been able to find where he was buried or who his parents were. Until we break through that "brick wall," the Martin line remains a dead end.

My efforts have been on becoming familiar with the basic features of the Website and sharing those with others. The Support Center and other resources are the next step for me. I found the *Unofficial Guide to Ancestry.com How To Find Your Family History On the #1 Genealogy Website* by Nancy Hendrickson useful. With my mostly German background, I expect to rely heavily on *Trace Your German Roots Online: A Complete Gide to German Genealogy Websites* by James M. Beidler.

I encourage you to join me in learning more.

NOTES

Section Four:
DNA Results & Subscription

Combining a Subscription with DNA Results allows you to view the trees of your DNA Matches. You may immediately see how you are related to a person if you find a recognizable relative in his or her tree.

Only after the DNA results arrived for my sister Ronda did I plunk down money for a Subscription. I had determined Ashley, my DNA match, and I did not share relatives on my maternal side. Ronda and I turned out to be half, not full, sisters. With a paid Subscription, I was able to open Ashley's small tree and there was a man, her grandfather, who by age and geographic location, might prove to be my biological father.

Discovering how I'm related to matches on my own is satisfying, but my favorite features, Shared Ancestor Hints and DNA Circles, sometimes do the work for me. DNA must be linked to a tree with pedigree ancestors (great-grandparents) added to the same tree. The software will then identify similar ancestors among people who share DNA.

Shared Ancestor Hints

A Shared Ancestor Hint indicates that you and a DNA Match have the same named ancestor listed in your respective trees. One of the benefits of Shared Ancestor Hints is that matches with small amounts of DNA are brought to your attention. I share only six cMs with someone who is a fifth cousin through our fourth-great-grandfather Philip Kochenderfer. Both of us spelled the name the same way, but small variations won't prevent the software from making the connection. The advantage for both was that her research complemented mine, and we were able to help each other fill gaps in our trees.

The green leaf hint indicating a Shared Ancestor is shown even when a tree is private. You won't be able to view the tree or see the relationship without an invitation. I message the match, asking them to send me the lineage information and almost always receive a response. Sometimes I receive a screenshot of the tree Kinship Diagram, and other times, get an invitation to view the match's tree.

Viewing Shared Ancestor Hints

Individually Shared Ancestors are indicated by a green leaf attached to the number of people in a match's tree.

1. Click on View Match of a DNA match who has such a green leaf hint.

2. The screen opens to Pedigree and Surname, showing how both you and the match trace back through your family lines to the common ancestor.

3. You may have more than one shared ancestor—look at the Shared Ancestor banner to see if there is a number and arrow indicating other shared ancestors.

4. Scroll down the page to view the complete tree.

Viewing ALL Shared Ancestor Hints

To avoid scrolling through hundreds of matches looking for those little green leaves, use this link:

1. On logging in, Ancestry.com opens to a screen with a Black Bar Menu across the top: HOME, TREES, SEARCH, DNA, HELP, EXTRAS

2. Choose DNA.

3. From the drop-down menu, click on Your DNA Results Summary.

4. The first link in the middle box – DNA Matches: Shared Ancestor Hints will indicate if you have shared matches.

DNA Circles

Each DNA Circle is a group of people who have the same pedigree ancestor (great-grandparents, not uncles or cousins) in their trees. Each person in the group has a DNA Match with at least one other person in the circle. I appreciate DNA Circles because they bring to my attention relatives who share only a small amount or no DNA with me. This helps me trace parts of my family who have migrated from Pennsylvania south and west.

The more ancestors you've included in your family tree, the more likely you are to have DNA Circles. According to Ancestry.com customer service, three or more people who share a common ancestor are needed to form a DNA Circle.

1. On logging in, Ancestry.com opens to a screen with a Black Bar Menu across the top: HOME, TREES, SEARCH, DNA, HELP, EXTRAS

2. Choose DNA Circles. If you don't have DNA Circles, first check to be sure your DNA is linked to your tree. Next spend time developing your tree using genealogical research.

3. If you do have DNA Circles, the screen opens to rectangles representing each Circle with the name of the most recent common ancestor and number of people in the circle.

4. Once you click to open the circle, you can

Spelling Variations

One of my early DNA Circles introduced matches who were related to me via my fourth-great-grandfather Philip Kochendorfer. Those living in Ohio spelled the name as Kochendarfer. The original name appears to have arrived in the US as Kochendoerfer. Small differences in spelling won't prevent Hints from appearing.

Trying to determine if a third-great-grandmother was Catharine, Catherine, or Katharine was a losing battle.

In some cases, the difference between an a or an o in a name makes a significant difference. Other times, not so much.

choose to see the people in their family groups called Relationships or as a List.

5. From here there are easily understood choices for viewing the matches and/or their trees.

You can learn who your recent (not ancient) genetic ancestors were from your DNA Circles. Inherited DNA carries back to approximately ten generations. I don't copy personal photos and documents from others. I do copy the names of my relatives from other trees, but only after confirming dates and relationships from census sheets and other public records. My tree grew and grew, up and out, as I added grandparents, their children, and siblings of both.

NOTES

Section Summaries
Untangling Costs/Services
for Genealogical Research & DNA Testing

The introductions from each section are summarized here to provide a quick overview of the costs and services available from Ancestry.com,

Section One: Guest Account — Creating & Sharing Trees

There is no cost for a guest account nor for creating and sharing family trees. Compare the features that are without cost in this section to the tree-viewing and research features described in Section Four.

Ancestry.com will send "Tree Hints" letting you know records are available for the people in your tree. You will eventually be directed to a screen with Subscription offers. If you are content with the features in this section, you can carry on indefinitely with a guest account.

Section Two: One-Time Cost For DNA Results

Anyone can buy any number of DNA Kits to use or give away. Once a kit is purchased there is no additional cost for activating the kit, the laboratory analysis, and additional features:
- DNA Matches
- Link DNA to your family tree
- Amount of DNA shared with matches
- Messaging system to communicate with matches
- Share DNA with others
- Migrations (previously Genetic Communities)
- Ethnicity Estimate

These are not "free." They are included in the cost of the kit, but this will help you understand why the features that combine DNA Results with public trees (e.g., Shared Ancestor Hints and DNA Circles) do have a cost. Viewing public trees requires a paid Subscription (Section Four).

Section Three: Subscription (Without DNA Results)

A paid Subscription provides access to public trees, unlocks the archives of record collections, and allows you to attach such documents to people in your family tree.

Many people choose never to participate in DNA testing. In other words, the price you pay for a Subscription is the same with or without DNA testing.

An Ancestry.com Subscription works similarly to a magazine Subscription. There is typically a discount price for first-time subscribers which increases to the standard rate upon renewal.

Section Four: DNA Results & Subscription

Combining a Subscription with DNA Results allows you to view the trees of your DNA Matches. If you have linked your DNA to a well-developed family tree, the software helps identify your DNA Matches through Shared Ancestor Hints and DNA Circles.

Genealogists who have had Subscriptions for years sometimes decide to submit DNA kits. It is not surprising that they will not know which features are a consequence of having received DNA Results and which require a Subscription. I hope this four-section format helped to clarify this issue.

NOTES

Resources for Learning about DNA Matching

Here are some of the books, articles, and websites I found useful.

DNAeXplained – Genetic Genealogy
      dna-explained.com
National Human Genome Research Institute
      www.genome.gov
International Society of Genetic Genealogy
      isogg.org
For information on endogamy
      isogg.org/wiki/Endogamy
The DNA Geek
      thednageek.com
The Genetic Genealogist
      thegeneticgenealogist.com
      (see the DNA chart with colored boxes)
Lisa Louise Cooke's Genealogy Gems
      https://lisalouisecooke.com
Ancestry White Papers
      https://tinyurl.com/ya8azhaz or search AncestryDNA White Papers
For additional sites, search online for DNA autosomal chart

NOTES

Glossary

This glossary was prepared specifically as an aid to reading this book. I have provided brief descriptions rather than exacting definitions. Website features for creating family trees and identifying DNA matches mostly refer to Ancestry.com. An online search of any of these terms will provide much more information.

Amount of DNA
Refers to the number of centiMorgans, which is a measure of shared DNA.

Ancestry
Merriam-Webster: line of descent, lineage. Synonyms: family tree, pedigree.

Ancestry.com
One of many companies that offers services related to DNA testing and researching family history. I used Ancestry.com (and GEDMatch.com) because their services met my needs. Additional companies are mentioned under Adoption Resources. Be sure the company you choose will suit your purposes.

AncestryDNA White Papers
Informative reports on the scientific background for many of Ancestry.com's features.

Black Bar Menu
Suggested starting point for navigation when using Ancestry.com's website. The Black Bar Menu runs across the top of the page with tabs for drop-down menus: HOME, TREES, SEARCH, DNA, HELP, EXTRAS

CentiMorgan(s)
Measure of shared DNA, shown as a number. Go to What is a CentiMorgan?

Confidence Levels for Shared DNA
The likelihood, represented by a percent, that shared genes were inherited (identical by descent—IBD). The alternative is that the shared genes happened by chance (IBS).

Confidence Score for Shared DNA
Ancestry.com converts confidence levels into words: extremely high, very high, high, good, moderate. The words indicate how likely the shared DNA listed was inherited.

DNA
Abbreviation for deoxyribonucleic acid, which is a nucleic acid that contains the genetic code. DNA is the carrier of genetic information—the building blocks of life.

DNA Matches
DNA Matches, all of whom have the same (shared / common) ancestor in their trees and share DNA with at least one other person in the group.

DNA Kit
Includes a tube for collecting spit, along with instructions for obtaining DNA Results.

DNA Matches
People who share DNA with you. Go to Section Two.

DNA Results
List of people who have also submitted kits and share DNA with you. There are features to help identify how you are related to unknown Matches. Ancestry.com also compares your DNA to other populations to obtain an estimate of where your ancient ancestors may have lived. Go to Sections Two & Four. See Migrations and Ethnicity Estimate.

Edit Relationships

Feature that allows you to link and/or unlink people in your tree without deleting them. Useful for fixing relationship mistakes and reconnecting people to the main tree.

Ethnicity Estimate

Probabilities your ancient ancestors came from a specified geographic area. See #20 Who Are We? and Ethnicity Estimate: Ancient Ancestors.

Family Tree

Diagram showing the relationships between generations in a family. Often used in this book to refer to online trees created on Ancestry.com's website. Go to Section One.

Family View

Graphical format (vertical) for viewing a tree in which family groups and their connections can be seen. Go to Section One.

Feature(s)

Term used to refer to a function which serves one or more purposes.

Gallery

A site accessed via a person's tree Profile View for uploading and/or viewing personal items.

Gene

Unit of heredity that is transferred from parent to offspring. A distinct sequence of nucleotides forming part of a chromosome.

Genealogists

Someone (lay or professional) who traces the pedigree lineages of families through historical and/or genetic research.

Genealogy

Study of family lineages through family history or genetics.

HELP: Support Center

Ancestry.com's "help desk" provides easily accessible, clearly written instructions with up-to-date screen shots. Go to HELP: Support Center.

Hierarchy / Hierarchically

Ordered by rank. For purposes here: DNA Matches, regardless of sort feature, are ranked in order by amount of DNA shared with you. Important when viewing the Shared Matches feature.

Identical by State (IBS)

Shared DNA is assumed to have happened by chance. Small segments of DNA are shared among populations which have no genealogical relevance.

Identical by Descent (IBD)

Shared DNA assumed to have been inherited (usually represented as a percent).

Kinship / Kinship Diagram

For our purposes, refers to family relationships: mother, uncle, brother, cousin, and so forth. I use "Kinship Diagram" to refer to the feature that shows how you are related to someone else in your tree.

Link DNA to tree

DNA can be linked to one person in one tree. DNA from more than one person can be linked to the same tree.

List of All People View

Format for viewing all people in a tree, under three headings: Name, Birth (date and place), and Death (date and place). Go to Section One.

Message(s) / Messaging system

Ancestry.com's internal system for registered users to communicate with each other.

Migrations

Ancestry.com's feature showing geographic clusters of recent ancestors (within ~ten generations) with whom you share DNA.

Most Recent Common Ancestor (MRCA)
Answers the question: How are we genetically related? The most recent—closest—person from whom you and a match inherited the DNA you share. Ancestry.com uses the term Shared Ancestor, who may or may not be the "most recent." I use shared and common interchangeably, but "most recent" is distinct. (E.g., Susan and I share / have in common many ancestors, but our MRCA is Irvin Martin.)

Pedigree View
Graphical format (horizontal) for viewing a tree in which a person and only his/her direct ancestors are seen. Go to Section One.

Profile View
Focuses on one person from a tree. His/her parents, siblings, spouse(s), and children are listed on one page. Go to Section One.

Do not confuse the tree Profile View mentioned often in this book with the "Ancestry Profile" page, which is not discussed. That page provides information about you to the public and is accessed via the drop-down menu from your account name on far right of Black Bar Menu.

Share DNA
Invite someone to view your DNA. A link to your DNA is placed in a registered user's account.

Share Family Tree(s)
Invite someone to view your tree. A link to your tree is placed in a registered user's account.

Shared Ancestor Hint
Green leaf (near a DNA Match) indicates a shared / common ancestor is in your tree and in the tree of the Match. Go to Section Four.

Shared DNA
Shown as a number and indicates the amount of DNA or centiMorgans you and a Match share.

Shared Matches (Triangulation)
Feature shows who, from your list of matches, shares DNA with you and another person. This may be only one person or can be many. Useful for identifying to which family lineage matches belong. Go to Section Two.

Software
I use the term to refer to Ancestry.com's manipulation of the data (e.g., members' DNA, names in trees). When we use various features, the software performs and the results are shown on the Website. It is important to remember that software performs according to rules. For example, the rule for privacy of living persons in a tree is not the absence of a death date, but a check mark for "Living." Knowing the rules can be useful for interpreting results.

Subscription
Provides access, for a fee, to view Ancestry.com public trees and record collections. Records can be attached to people in your family tree. See Sections Three & Four.

Support Center
Ancestry.com provides easily accessible, clearly written instructions with up-to-date screenshots. Go to HELP: Support Center.

Tree Hint
Green leaf (on name box of a person in a family tree) indicates records are available that may pertain to the person. Hints can be accessed via the Profile View. Go to Section Four.

Triangulation
Used here to refer to the process of identifying family relationships with the Shared Matches feature. Go to Section Two.

Website / website
For use here, pages (or screens) available online, maintained by an organization. When referring to Ancestry.com's website, Website is capitalized.

INDEX